Well Said
Intro

Linda Grant

HEINLE
CENGAGE Learning™

Australia • Brazil • Japan • Korea • Mexico • Singapore • Spain • United Kingdom • United States

Well Said Intro
Linda Grant

Publisher, Adult & Academic ESL: James W. Brown
Senior Acquisitions Editor: Sherrise Roehr
Director of Product Development: Anita Raducanu
Director of Product Marketing: Amy Mabley
Product Marketing Manager: Laura Needham
Senior Field Marketing Manager: Donna Lee Kennedy
Assistant Marketing Manager: Caitlin Driscoll
Associate Development Editor: Katherine Carroll
Editorial Assistant: Katherine Reilly
Production Editor: Chrystie Hopkins
Print Buyer: Betsy Donaghey
Production Services:
   LaurelTech Integrated Publishing Services
Cover Designer: Gina Petti/Rotunda Design House
Printer: Edwards Brothers
Cover Image: © Malevich, Zazimir. Suprematism no. 50.
© Art Resource, NY.

Illustration Credits
Chapter 5 Page 35: © The New Yorker Collection 1994
Jack Ziegler from cartoonbank.com. All rights reserved.
Chapter 6 Page 46: – Just Pik't Orange Juice Carton,
Reprinted with permission of Orchid Island Juice
Chapter 8 Page 72: CALVIN AND HOBBES © (1987)
Watterson. Dist. By UNIVERSAL PRESS SYNDICATE.
Reprinted with permission. All rights reserved.
Page 74: © The New Yorker Collection 2002 Tom Cheney
from cartoonbank.com. All rights reserved.
Chapter 10 Page 91: ZIGGY © (2003) ZIGGY AND
FRIENDS, INC. Reprinted with permission of
UNIVERSAL PRESS SYNDICATE. All rights reserved.
Chapter 11 Page 105: ZIGGY © (2002) ZIGGY AND
FRIENDS, INC. Reprinted with permission of
UNIVERSAL PRESS SYNDICATE. All rights reserved.
Chapter 12 Page 116: CALVIN AND HOBBES © (1992)
Watterson. Dist. By UNIVERSAL PRESS SYNDICATE.
Reprinted with permission. All rights reserved.
Chapter 14 Page 141: © Mark Parisi, printed with
permission.
Photo Credits
Chapter 8 Page 76: © Janine Wiedel Photolibrary /
Alamy
Print Permissions:
Chapter 9 Page 80: "Hi. How Are You Today?", from THE
BUTTERFLY JAR by Jeff Moss, copyright © 1989 by Jeff
Moss. Use by permission of Bantam Books, a division of
Random House, Inc.
Chapter 9 Page 88: "This is Just to Say" By William
Carlos Williams, from COLLECTED POEMS: 1909-1939,
VOLUME I, copyright © 1983 by New Directions
Publishing Corp. Reprinted by permission of New
Directions Publishing Corp.

For permission to use material from
this text or product, submit all requests online at
cengage.com/permissions
Further permissions questions can be emailed to
permissionrequest@cengage.com

Library of Congress Control Number: 2005934880

ISBN 13: 978-1-4130-0510-3
ISBN 10: 1-4130-0510-1
ISBN: 1-4130-1546-8 (International Student Edition)

Heinle
25 Thomson Place
Boston, MA 02110.

Cengage Learning is a leading provider of customized
learning solutions with office locations around the globe,
including Singapore, the United Kingdom, Australia,
Mexico, Brazil and Japan. Locate your local office at:
international.cengage.com/region

Cengage Learning products are represented in Canada
by Nelson Education, Ltd.

Visit Heinle online at **elt.heinle.com**
Visit our corporate website at **cengage.com**

Printed in the United States of America.
3 4 5 6 7 8 9 10 — 10 09 08

Contents

Pronunciation Symbol Guide v
To the Instructor vii
Acknowledgments x
To the Student xi

PART 1

Unit 1: Getting Started

Chapter 1: Your Pronunciation Needs 1
Chapter 2: Setting Goals 7
Chapter 3: Syllables and Dictionary Basics 11

Unit 2: Word Endings

Chapter 4: Final Consonant Sounds and Linking 21
Chapter 5: Syllables and -s Endings 31
Chapter 6: Syllables and -ed Endings 43

Unit 3: Stress in Words

Chapter 7: Stressed Syllables—Numbers, Nouns, and Verbs 53
Chapter 8: Stressed Syllables—Suffixes 67

Unit 4: Rhythm in Sentences

Chapter 9: Basic Rhythm—Stressed Words 79
Chapter 10: Basic Rhythm—Reduced Words 89

Unit 5: Intonation in Discourse

Chapter 11: Focus Words 99
Chapter 12: Intonation: Rising and Falling 113
Chapter 13: Thought Groups and Pausing 123

Unit 6: Sound Change in Connected Speech

Chapter 14: Connected Speech 133

PART 2 Consonant and Vowel Supplements

Consonant Introduction
Supplement 1: Phonetic Alphabet. 147
Supplement 2: Consonant Overview. 149
Supplement 3: Selecting Consonant Sounds to Study 156

Consonant Practices
Supplement 4: Initial /p/ **pie**–/b/ **buy**, /t/ **time**–/d/ **dime**, /k/ **cold**–/g/ **gold** . . 157
Supplement 5: Final /p/ **cap**–/b/ **cab**, /t/ **seat**–/d/ **seed**, /k/ **back**–/g/ **bag** . . 163
Supplement 6: /m/ **some**–/n/ **sun**–/ŋ/ **sung** 166
Supplement 7: /θ/ **thin** 170
Supplement 8: /ʃ/ **sheep**–/tʃ/ **cheap**–/dʒ/ **jeep** 174
Supplement 9: /l/ **light**–/r/ **right** 178

Consonant Cluster Practice
Supplement 10: Initial Consonant Clusters (**play** vs. **pay**) 181
Supplement 11: Final Consonant Clusters (**fast** vs. **fat**) 184

Vowel Introduction
Supplement 12: Phonetic Alphabet. 187
Supplement 13: Vowel Overview 188
Supplement 14: Selecting Vowel Sounds to Study 194

Vowel Practices
Supplement 15: /iʸ/ **heat**–/ɪ/ **hit**. 195
Supplement 16: /eʸ/ **late**–/ɛ/ **let**. 199
Supplement 17: /uʷ/ **too**–/ʊ/ **took**. 203
Supplement 18: /æ/ **cap**–/ʌ/ **cup**–/ɑ/ **cop** 207

Information Gap Activities. **211**
Appendix 1: Personal Key Word List. **213**
Appendix 2: Common Words with Omitted Syllables **214**
Appendix 3: Suffixes and Word Stress **214**
Appendix 4: Feedback Form—Giving Instructions **215**
Answer Key: Prime-Time Practices. **216**
Answer Key: Consonant Supplements **217**
Answer Key: Vowel Supplements **223**
Index **227**

GUIDE TO SYMBOLS in *Well Said Intro*

CONSONANTS

KEY WORD	SYMBOL		KEY WORD	SYMBOL
pie	/p/		**sh**oe	/ʃ/
boy	/b/		mea**s**ure	/ʒ/
ten	/t/		**ch**oose	/tʃ/
day	/d/		**j**ob	/dʒ/
key	/k/		**m**y	/m/
go	/g/		**n**o	/n/
fine	/f/		si**ng**	/ŋ/
van	/v/		**l**et	/l/
see	/s/		**r**ed	/r/
zoo	/z/		**w**e	/w/
think	/θ/		**y**es	/y/
they	/ð/		**h**ome	/h/

VOWELS

KEY WORD	SYMBOL		KEY WORD	SYMBOL
h**e**	/iʸ/		t**oo**	/uʷ/
h**i**t	/ɪ/		g**oo**d	/ʊ/
m**ay**	/eʸ/		kn**ow**	/oʷ/
g**e**t	/ɛ/		l**aw**	/ɔ/
m**a**d	/æ/		f**i**ne	/aɪ/
b**ir**d	/ɜr/		n**ow**	/aʊ/
c**u**p	/ʌ/		b**oy**	/ɔɪ/
about	/ə/			
h**o**t	/ɑ/			

GUIDE TO SYMBOLS in *Well Said Intro*

STRESS and RHYTHM	In a *word*, the syllable with the main stress is capitalized. In a *sentence,* the stressed words are capitalized.	SCI ence sci en TIF ic I can GIVE you a RIDE. I CAN'T GIVE you a RIDE.
FOCUS	In a phrase or sentence, the word that gets the *most* stress—the focus—is in capital letters and has a dot over it. Sometimes the focus is in capital letters and in bold type.	It's C·OLD. You NEED a ·COAT. It's **COLD**. You NEED a **COAT**.
INTONATION	An arrow points down if the pitch falls. An arrow points up if the pitch rises.	It's a BEAUtiful DAY, ISn't it.↘ You're from CHIna, AREn't you?↗
PHRASING	The end of a phrase or thought group is marked with a slash.	He doesn't like his students/arriving late.
LINKING	A link shows that the end of one word connects to the beginning of the next word.	Sit‿down. Wake‿up!

To the Instructor

Well Said Intro is a lower-level companion for *Well Said: Pronunciation for Clear Communication*. This introductory text targets high-beginning to mid-intermediate level learners of English. It is designed for students who have a fundamental level of functional oral communication and can attend to basic, high-priority pronunciation details.

The text is designed to improve the pronunciation and overall communicative effectiveness of students in a variety of instructional programs including two-year college, intensive English, international teaching assistant, and adult education.

The materials are appropriate as a primary text in a quarter- or semester-length pronunciation or pronunciation/speaking course; as a supplementary text in an oral communication, speech communication, or all-skills course; as the basis for individual or small group tutorials; and, as a program for self-study.

Well Said Intro introduces basic pronunciation features for intensive study and practice. *Well Said: Pronunciation for Clear Communication* recycles and spirals these features in more challenging contexts. The two-level series increases the likelihood that high-priority pronunciation concepts are internalized and become automatic.

FEATURES THAT UNITE *WELL SAID INTRO* AND *WELL SAID*
- focused listening tasks
- integration with naturalistic speaking formats
- emphasis on stress/rhythm/intonation as well as troublesome consonants and vowels
- multi-sensory/multi-modality approaches to pronunciation instruction with an emphasis on aural, visual, and kinesthetic modes
- gradual transition from controlled practice (with a focus on form) to engaging, relevant communicative speaking tasks (with a focus on meaning)
- field activities which move practice out of the classroom and into real-world speaking contexts
- homework activities that encourage rehearsal and self-monitoring
- student text/audio package for self- and/or individualized study

FEATURES THAT DISTINGUISH *WELL SAID INTRO*
Several new features are prompted by learner needs at the high-beginning/intermediate level, intervening trends in pronunciation, and gaps in available materials. In addition to shorter chapters, more accessible vocabulary, more basic and concrete speaking contexts, more controlled practice with a focus on group repetition, these key additions make this lower level text distinct:

- **Focus on Awareness-Raising and "Noticing":** This basic text emphasizes the first stage in pronunciation change—awareness-raising. It accomplishes this through *Get Set!*, an interactive segment opening each chapter. *Get Set!* draws the learners' attention to the specific feature under study and how it fulfills communicative functions in English. The more obvious these connections, the less explanation is required and the more motivated learners will be.

- **Use of Corpus Data:** Vocabulary comes from lists of the most common words as well as from Coxhead's Academic Word List. When placing words in thought groups or in contexts for linking, corpus data (e.g., Collins Cobuild Concordance and Collocations Sampler) was used in an effort to include frequently co-occurring lexical items or frequent word combinations.

- **Integration of Segmentals and Suprasegmentals:** Even though suprasegmentals (stress, rhythm, and intonation) appear in the chapters and segmentals (consonants and vowels) appear as supplements, *You Choose!* boxes are placed in chapters where a vowel or consonant supplement can be effectively integrated. In this way, the text points out those places where the segmental and suprasegmental systems intersect. Also, teachers can integrate vowel and consonant supplements according to the needs of a particular class or suggest a specific supplement according to the needs of an individual student.

- **Recognition of English as a Global Language:** The next generation of pronunciation texts need to consider English pronunciation in the expanding international context. Although the predominant pronunciation models in this project are speakers of North American English (NAE), the voice talent includes speakers of other varieties of English. This recognizes that English is a global language with a variety of accents and dialects.

Although the high-priority pronunciation features in this text include those that contribute to intelligibility in native speaker–nonnative speaker interactions, a teacher or student can also select many features that contribute to mutual intelligibility in nonnative speaker–non-native speaker interactions in English (based on research by Jenkins, 2000, OUP).

COMPONENTS
- Student Text with Index and Answer Keys for Supplements (Part 2)
- Instructor's Manual with Answer Keys for Chapters 1-14 (Part 1)
- Audio Program: The numbers inside the headset icon $\binom{}{1, 1}$ in the student text show the CD or cassette number and track number, respectively.

OVERALL ORGANIZATION OF THE TEXT
The Table of Contents shows that the focus of the text moves from stress in words—to rhythm in sentences—to intonation in connected speech. From the very beginning of the text, however, practice is contextualized into phrases, sentences, and longer stretches of speech. In addition, practice is recycled and spiraled throughout the text.

The Table of Contents also indicates that Part 1 of the text concentrates on suprasegmentals (stress, rhythm, intonation, thought groups); Part 2 of the text, the supplements, concentrates on segmentals (consonant and vowel sounds). However, segmentals are integrated into Part 1 and vice-versa.

See the Introduction to the Instructor's Manual for a more detailed description of each unit, as well as information about the diagnostic and goal setting tools in Chapters 1 and 2.

HEADINGS WITHIN CHAPTERS

In *Well Said Intro*, practice in each chapter moves from less-controlled to more-controlled and back to less-controlled. Each chapter has an hourglass structure, starting with the feature in a meaningful context (wide lens), zooming in on perception and production of the form (narrow lens), and then re-seating the feature in a relevant, meaningful communicative context (wide lens).

GET SET! raises awareness of the target feature through an interactive speaking activity.

LISTEN! helps learners strengthen their perception of the target feature.

In RULES AND PRACTICES, students discover basic rules of thumb. Then they practice the target feature in a variety of controlled and semi-controlled exercises.

In COMMUNICATIVE PRACTICE, students engage in intermediate level speaking tasks designed to elicit the target features.

In EXTEND YOUR SKILLS, target features are recycled into oral presentations, explanations, and other real-world speaking tasks.

ADDITIONAL SEGMENTS WITHIN CHAPTERS

Pronunciation to Go! helps students transfer pronunciation skills to everyday English.

Prime-Time Practice is homework that builds self-sufficiency through dictionary and self-monitoring assignments.

A Helpful Hint! and *Something to Think About!* are sidebars that describe pronunciation and communication strategies.

You Choose! boxes allow classes to continue with the chapter or integrate suggested supplements from Part 2.

ACKNOWLEDGMENTS

I would like to thank the following reviewers for their ideas and helpful suggestions regarding *Well Said Intro*:

Tony Carnerie
University of California San Diego, La Jolla, CA, United States

Miranda Childe
Miami Dade College, Miami, FL, United States

Anne Delaney
University of California San Diego, La Jolla, CA, United States

Liz Kelley
University of California San Diego, La Jolla, CA, United States

Jan McTyre
University of California San Diego Extension, San Diego, CA, United States

Richard Sansone
Valencia Community College, Orlando, FL, United States

Kelly Smith
University of California San Diego, La Jolla, CA, United States

I am grateful to Judy Gilbert for creating communities for the exchange of ideas about pronunciation; to Karen Tucker and Linda Gajdusek for valuable feedback on drafts of the text; to Cheryl Benz for allowing me to teach and pilot materials at Georgia Perimeter College; to Janet Goodwin, Cathy Jacobson, and Sue Miller for being supportive colleagues and friends; to Jane McNabb for her title *Pronunciation To Go!*; and to Chiaki Kajiro for her idea of stretching rubber bands vertically to practice focus.

Special appreciation to Jim Brown, Sherrise Roehr, Katie Carroll, and Chrystie Hopkins, editors at Thomson Heinle, for their patience and support.

A final thanks to my Burmese cat, Seal, who has been my constant companion throughout the entire writing process, though I regret to say her pronunciation has not improved one bit. And to my husband, Jim, who hardly ever says *no*.

To the Student

This text gives you the tools to speak English clearly. Speaking clearly means two things. It means listeners can understand what *you* say. It also means that you can understand what *others* say.

Here are answers to common questions about speaking clearly:

Q: Do I need to lose my accent?

    A: You do not need to lose your accent. You can speak English that is clear, but accented.

Q: How will this book help me improve my pronunciation?

    A: This text will teach basic pronunciation features. Basic pronunciation features are those that interfere the most with clear speaking.

    First, you might not **hear** pronunciation differences between your language and English. This book will help you notice those differences.

    The text will also help you **speak** more clearly. You will practice new sounds and patterns. You will practice in structured exercises. And you will practice in more typical everyday communication.

    Finally, you will learn to **self-monitor**. That means you will record, listen to, and correct your own speech.

Q: How long will it take to improve my pronunciation?

    A: That depends on the individual.

    Is your language very different from English? Then your progress may be a little slower.

    Are you truly motivated? Then your progress may be a little faster.

    Have you been speaking English for a long time? Then your habits may be hard to break.

    Do not get discouraged. Practice regularly. Use the tools in this book. And your pronunciation will gradually improve.

Q: What are some normal stages of learning?

A: Many students experience the following stages, but not necessarily in this order:

You become **aware** of the new sound pattern. You start to hear it in the speech of others.

You can **say** it correctly—but only when you are **thinking** about it.

Sometimes you think your speech is getting **worse**, not better. (Do not worry. Mistakes are a necessary, normal part of the process.)

In time, you can **say** the new sound pattern **automatically**. Maybe you don't use it 100 percent of the time. Maybe you use a new sound only 50 percent of the time. Even then, your speech will be clearer and much improved!

As time goes on, your use of the new pattern increases.

Q: Sometimes non-native speakers understand me when I speak English, but native speakers do not. Why?

A: Your language has unique sound and rhythm patterns. The patterns are different from English patterns. But they are similar to patterns in other languages. If you speak English with rhythm patterns from your native language, they may be familiar to other non-native speakers but not to English speakers.

This text will help you learn what a native English-speaking listener needs to understand you. But remember there is more than one effective way to speak English. It depends on who your listener is.

Q: How can I speed up my progress?

A: Your progress will depend on YOU—how **motivated** you are, how clear you want or need to be in your daily life, how much you **practice**, and how much you **communicate** in English **outside of class!**

Good Luck. I hope you enjoy this text and find it useful.

Linda Grant

Your Pronunciation Needs

In this chapter, you will learn

- How you can improve your pronunciation

Speaking Activities

Complete one or more of these activities. They will give your teacher a general idea of your pronunciation ability.

Part 1 Read a Paragraph

Part 2 Finish a Picture Story

Part 3 Answer Questions

You can make an appointment with your teacher or make a recording. You may submit the recording on a CD or cassette tape or send a voice file by e-mail.

Your teacher can use the Pronunciation Checklist on page 6 to record observations. At the end of the course, measure your progress by repeating one or two of the speaking activities.

Part 1 Reading a Paragraph

Look over the paragraph to see if you understand it. Do you have any questions? If not, read the paragraph out loud. Speak as naturally as possible.

1   What is the goal of pronunciation? Do you need to sound like a

2   native speaker? Do you have to lose your accent to be understood?

3   When setting goals, think about the situations in which you speak

4   English. For example, if you use the telephone at work, your

5   pronunciation needs to be very clear. In casual conversations with

6   friends or classmates, your speech can be more relaxed.

7   In general, it is important to be realistic. You do not need perfect

8   pronunciation. You can speak with an accent and still be clear. In this

9   course, you will learn which pronunciation features help your listener

10   the most. You will also learn that changing pronunciation is gradual.

11   It takes time, patience, and motivation.

Part 2 Finishing a Picture Story

Look at the picture story below. Read the first part of the story. Finish it in your own words.

Richard and Sara work for a software company. Last Friday, they finished a big project. They decided to celebrate by going to a movie.

At the theater, Richard suggested they see the vampire movie. Sara said, "I don't like vampire movies. I can't stand the sight of blood." Richard told her not to worry. He said, "You can hold my hand."

(Now use the pictures to finish the story.)

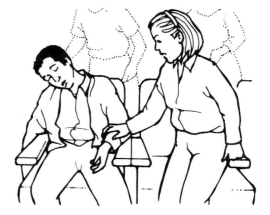

Part 3 Answering Questions

Choose one or two of the questions below. Answer each question in about one minute. Speak as naturally as possible.

A. What were you doing three years ago?

B. What would you like to be doing in five years?

C. In what situations do you speak English?

In-class Speaking Activity—Interview and Introduce a Classmate

Part A Interview your partner. Take notes below. (Your partner should close the book while being interviewed.)

Interview Questions	Notes
What is your first and last name?	
Do you have a nickname?	
What languages do you speak?	
Who is in your family? Where do your family members live?	
What is your major area of study? (or) What kind of work do you do?	
What do you do in your free time? What are your interests?	
What are three adjectives that describe you?	
What is the best advice you ever received?	
One more question:	

Part B Introduce your partner to the class. Use this outline to plan your introduction. You might begin by saying, "My name is _____ and I'd like to introduce _____."

Notes

1. Name:

2. Languages:

3. Area of study (if a student):

   Work or Occupation (if not a student):

4. Three most interesting pieces of information:

   a.

   b.

   c.

As you listen to your classmates introduce their partners, write the following:

Two things that made the speakers *easy* to understand:	Two things that made the speakers *hard* to understand:
1. _____	1. _____
2. _____	2. _____

PRONUNCIATION CHECKLIST (*To be completed by the instructor*)

Name _____ Date _____

Check features that need improvement:

Features	Examples	Chapter/Supplement
❑ **1.** Stress in Words		Chapters 7 and 8
❑ **2.** General Rhythm		Chapters 9 and 10
❑ **3.** Focus (emphasizing most important words)		Chapters 11 and 12
❑ **4.** Rising and Falling Intonation		Chapter 12
❑ **5.** Phrasing and Pausing; Linking		Chapter 13 Chapters 4 and 14
❑ **6.** Final Consonant Sounds; *-s* and *-ed* Endings		Chapter 4 Chapters 5 and 6
❑ **7.** Initial Consonant Clusters; Final Consonant Clusters		Supplement 10 Supplement 11
❑ **8.** Difficult Consonants		Supplements 4–11
❑ **9.** Difficult Vowels		Supplements 12–18

General Delivery:

10. Loudness	appropriate	1—2—3	too soft/too loud
11. Speed	appropriate	1—2—3	too fast/too slow
12. Eye Contact	appropriate	1—2—3	inappropriate

Strengths: **Needs:**
1.   1.
2.   2.
3.   3.

Setting Goals

In this chapter, you will

- Learn about pronunciation basics
- Think about how pronunciation affects communication
- Set personal goals for the course

Task 1   Write short answers:

1. Have you ever listened to people who do *not* speak *your* native language well?

   What makes them *hard* to understand? What makes them *easy* to understand?

2. What makes native speakers of English *hard* to understand? What makes them *easy* to understand?

Discuss your answers in a small group. Choose one person to lead the discussion and another person to report to the class.

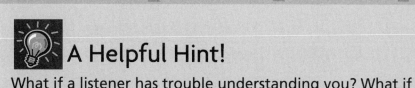

A Helpful Hint!

What if a listener has trouble understanding you? What if a listener is not familiar with your accent? How can you help?

1. S-l-o-w down.

2. Pause between phrases.

Always do these two things. You will be easier to understand immediately.

Task 2 Write three words or phrases that are difficult for you to say. What do you think the problem is?

1. Word/Phrase _____   Problem _____

2. Word/Phrase _____   Problem _____

3. Word/Phrase _____   Problem _____

Task 3 Look at these **pronunciation basics**. See the **examples** of how they can affect communication. What is your **ability** in each area? If you are not sure, **guess**.

Pronounciation Basics	Example	Ability (poor 1-2-3-4 good)
1. Every word has one syllable that is the strongest.	HIS-tor-y If you give all syllables the same stress, the listener might hear *his story*!	1—2—3—4
2. More important words are strong; less important words are weak.	JOHN can DRIVE. If you make all words strong, the listener might hear *John can't drive!*	1—2—3—4
3. Divide speech into phrases.	How is your daughter,/ Mary? If you use one phrase instead of two, it will sound like *Mary* is the daughter's name.	1—2—3—4
4. Emphasize the most important word in every phrase by changing the pitch of your voice.	Did you lose the **HOUSE** key /or **CAR** key? If you emphasize *key,* you will call attention to less important words.	1—2—3—4
5. Final sounds are important.	He lets me borrow his card. What if you omit the *–s* and *–d?* The listener might think you *borrowed* a car.	1—2—3—4
6. Consonant sounds	Difficulties with consonants vary by language group and individual.	1—2—3—4
7. Vowel sounds	Difficulties with vowels vary by language group and individual.	1—2—3—4

Which pronunciation basics do you think you need the **most** help with?

a.   b.   c.

Something to Think About!

Many students think they need the most practice with consonants and vowels. Although consonant and vowel sounds are important, stress, rhythm, and intonation are important too!

Have you ever seen a food pyramid? For a healthy diet, you have to eat from all the food groups. Pronunciation is like that too. For clear speaking, you have to practice all the pronunciation features.

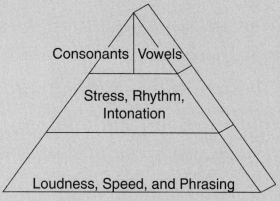

▲ **Figure 2-1** Pronunciation Pyramid.

Start at the top of the pyramid. Imagine that your consonants and vowels are accurate, but your stress, rhythm, and intonation are *not* clear. You will be hard to understand.

Now imagine that your consonants, vowels, stress, rhythm, and intonation are all clear, but you speak too softly, too quickly, or without pauses. You still will be hard to understand!

Task 4 Why do you want to improve your English? For work, school, travel, or pleasure? In what situations do you want to speak clearly and effectively? Circle your reasons.

talking on the telephone	speaking at meetings
casual conversations with friends	teaching in English
talking with co-workers	giving short reports
asking/answering questions in class	participating in discussions
talking with nonnative speakers of English	other?

In a small group, make a list of the most frequent situations. Then report to the class.

Situation 1. _____

Situation 2. _____

Task 5 Set personal goals for the course. Use the scale below.

1. How clear is your speech now? Check (✓) your current pronunciation level.

2. How clear do you want your speech to be or need it to be? Star (✱) your goal.

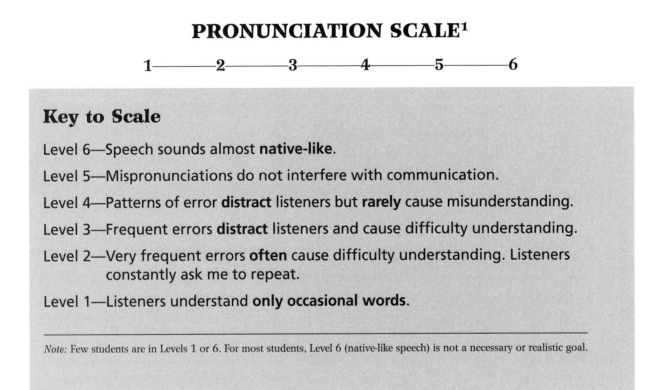

PRONUNCIATION SCALE[1]

1———2———3———4———5———6

Key to Scale

Level 6—Speech sounds almost **native-like**.

Level 5—Mispronunciations do not interfere with communication.

Level 4—Patterns of error **distract** listeners but **rarely** cause misunderstanding.

Level 3—Frequent errors **distract** listeners and cause difficulty understanding.

Level 2—Very frequent errors **often** cause difficulty understanding. Listeners constantly ask me to repeat.

Level 1—Listeners understand **only occasional words**.

Note: Few students are in Levels 1 or 6. For most students, Level 6 (native-like speech) is not a necessary or realistic goal.

3. Did your teacher check (✓) your pronunciation level? What was your teacher's evaluation?

[1] Scale adapted from Pronunciation Proficiency Continuum, Grant, L., *Well Said: Pronunciation for Clear Communication*, Boston: Heinle and Heinle, 2001:7. Scale based on Morley, J., "ESL/EFL Intelligibility Index," in How Many Languages Do You Speak? Nagoya Gakuin Daigaku: Gaikokugo Kyoiku Kiyo No. 19, Jan./Feb. 1988.

Syllables and Dictionary Basics

A syllable is a part of a word. Syllables are the building blocks of English.

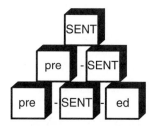

Dictionaries tell you what a word means. They also answer basic questions about the pronunciation of a word.

How many syllables or beats does a word have?

1, 1 Words have one, two, three, or more syllables or beats. Listen.

1 Syllable	2 Syllables	3 Syllables
tea	ta · co	to · ma · to
quite	qui · et	qui · et · ly

Now say the words *with* your teacher or the speaker on the audio.

1, 2 Each syllable has a vowel sound. The word *taco* has two vowel sounds and two syllables—*ta · co*. Listen and say the words with your teacher or the speaker on the audio. Tap the boxes as you say each syllable.

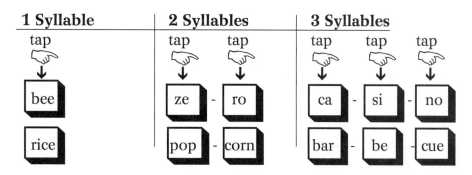

Exercise 1 Listen to the teacher or the speaker on the audio say each pair of words. Are the number of syllables the same (S) or different (D)? Circle S or D.

			Same	Different
Examples: black	blue		Ⓢ	D
	box	boxes	S	Ⓓ
1. ten	home		S	D
2. act	actor		S	D
3. quiet	broken		S	D
4. bank	basic		S	D
5. forget	decide		S	D
6. decide	decided		S	D
7. begin	introduce		S	D
8. Korea	vanilla		S	D

Check your answers. Listen again.

Exercise 2 Listen. Check the word you hear.

1 Syllable	**2 Syllables**
Example: ✓ cook	___ cookie
1. ___ planned	___ planet
2. ___ say	___ essay
3. ___ sit	___ city
4. ___ stopped	___ stop it
5. ___ small	___ some mall

2 Syllables	**3 Syllables**
6. ✓ center	___ senator
7. ___ present	___ president
8. ___ explained	___ explain it
9. ___ omit	___ omitted
10. ___ tasted	___ tasted it

Check your answers.
Now listen to the speaker say each pair. Tap for each syllable.

Something to Think About!

Omitting syllables may confuse your listener.

Example:	We **need-ed** it.	4 syllables = *past*
	We **need** it.	3 syllables = *present*

Adding syllables may confuse your listener.

Example:	Where's the stu-dent **cen- ter**?	6 syllables = *place*
	Where's the stu-dent **sen-a-tor**?	7 syllables = *person*

Do not omit or add syllables if you want your meaning to be clear.*

---

*Syllables are omitted in certain English words like *family, vegetable*, and *chocolate*. See Appendix 2 for a more complete list.

Exercise 3 With your partner, guess how many syllables or beats each word or phrase has.

Syllables

Example: potato	3
1. desk	
2. menu	
3. clock	
4. magazine	
5. umbrella	
6. forty	
7. needed	
8. needed it	
9. stopped	
10. stopped it	

Check your answers.

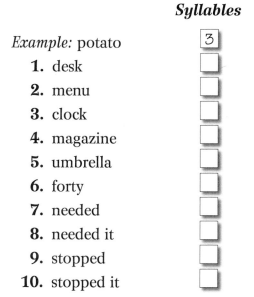 Now listen to the teacher or the speaker on the audio say each word/phrase.

Most dictionaries separate syllables with dots.

↓

sen•a•tor /ˈsɛ-nə-tər/ *n.*

The word *senator* has three syllables.

Exercise 4 These are some of the most beautiful words in the English language, according to a recent survey.* Listen.

Most Beautiful English Words

banana	hope	mother	bubble
sweetheart	sunshine	blue	sunflower
fantastic	rainbow	kangaroo	peace
pumpkin	freedom	umbrella	moment
twinkle	if	liberty	gum

What do *you* think? What five words do you think are the most beautiful words in English? Use words from the box or think of your own. Write the number of syllables. Check your dictionary if you are not sure.

	Words	Syllables
1.	_____	___
2.	_____	___
3.	_____	___
4.	_____	___
5.	_____	___

Share your words with a partner and then with the class.

Optional: In a small group, list English words that do not sound pleasant. Write the number of syllables.

	Words	Syllables
1.	_____	___
2.	_____	___
3.	_____	___

You will learn more about syllables in Chapters 5 and 6.

---

*The survey was conducted in 2004 by the British Council. It polled more than 7,000 English language students in 46 countries.

Which syllable is the strongest?

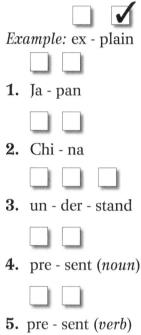

In words with two or more syllables, one syllable is stronger than the others. Listen.

2 Syllables	3 Syllables	4 Syllables
TU · na	RE · ci · pe	av · o · CA · do
ca · REER	suc · CESS · ful	e · CON · o · my

Exercise 5 You will hear each word two times. Check (✔) the box with the strongest syllable.

☐ ✔

Example: ex - plain

☐ ☐

1. Ja - pan

☐ ☐

2. Chi - na

☐ ☐ ☐

3. un - der - stand

☐ ☐

4. pre - sent (*noun*)

☐ ☐

5. pre - sent (*verb*)

Check your answers.

Now say each word two times *with* the teacher or the speaker on the audio.

Dictionaries show stressed syllables. Most dictionaries put a mark (') before the syllable with the main or primary stress.

The first syllable has primary stress when *present* is a noun. *(n.)*

↓

pre•sent /ˈprɛ-zənt/ *n.*

The second syllable has primary stress when *present* is a verb. *(v.)*

↓

pre•sent /prɪ-ˈzɛnt/ *v.*

Exercise 6 With your partner, guess the syllable with primary stress. Then check your dictionary and mark the primary stress. Use *your* dictionary or the online *Newbury House Dictionary* at http://elt.thomson.com/nhd.

Guess the primary stress	*Check your dictionary*
☑ ☐	
Example: cof fee	**'**cof fee
☐ ☐	
1. po lice	po lice
☐ ☐	
2. fi nal	fi nal
☐ ☐	
3. pro mise	pro mise
☐ ☐ ☐ ☐	
4. a bil i ty	a bil i ty
☐ ☐ ☐	
5. pi an o	pi an o

Check your answers.
Say each word after your teacher or the speaker on the audio.

1, 12

💡 A Helpful Hint!

Words with three or more syllables sometimes have three levels of stress.

1. /**'**/strong or primary stress
2. /ˌ/light or secondary stress
3. no stress

Example: ˌap · pli · **'**ca · tion

Pay special attention to the syllable with primary stress.

Exercise 7 Write three words that are difficult for you to say. You may use words from Task 2 in Chapter 2 (page 8). Look up the words in your dictionary. Mark the syllable with primary stress. Write a sentence you would say using the word.

Example: Mei works as a server in a restaurant. She often asks her customers if they would like dessert.

_____des 'sert_____   _____Would you like dessert?_____

1. _____   _____

2. _____   _____

3. _____   _____

Report your words and sentences to a small group.

You will learn more about stress in words in Chapters 7 and 8.

Do words sound the way they are spelled?

Not always. That is why dictionaries use special symbols for pronunciation. The word *cough* has five letters but only three symbols or sounds.

5 letters   3 symbols or sounds
   ↓   ↓

cough /kɔf/ *v.*

Exercise 8 Are these word pairs pronounced the same? With your partner, check your dictionary. If the symbols are *exactly* the same, the words sound the same. If the symbols are different, the words sound different.

					Same	*Different*
Examples:	son	/sʌn/	sun	/sʌn/	✔	☐
	pool	/puʷl/	pull	/pʊl/	☐	✔
1. war			wore		☐	☐
2. throw			through		☐	☐
3. clothes			close (*verb*)		☐	☐
4. loose			lose		☐	☐
5. wood			would		☐	☐

Check your answers.
Listen to the teacher or the speaker on the audio say each pair.

🎧 1, 13

How do I pronounce the symbols?

Symbols vary from dictionary to dictionary. Check the Pronunciation Guide or Key in *your* dictionary.

Pronunciation Key

The symbols in *Well Said Intro* are the same as the symbols in the *Newbury House Dictionary* except for four vowel symbols. Can you find them?

CONSONANT SYMBOLS

Key Word	Well Said	Newbury	Your Dictionary
1. **p**ie	/p/	/p/	
2. **b**oy	/b/	/b/	
3. **t**en	/t/	/t/	
4. **d**ay	/d/	/d/	
5. **k**ey	/k/	/k/	
6. **g**o	/g/	/g/	
7. **f**ine	/f/	/f/	
8. **v**an	/v/	/v/	
9. **th**ink	/θ/	/θ/	
10. **th**ey	/ð/	/ð/	
11. **s**ee	/s/	/s/	
12. **z**oo	/z/	/z/	
13. **sh**oe	/ʃ/	/ʃ/	
14. mea**s**ure	/ʒ/	/ʒ/	
15. **ch**oose	/tʃ/	/tʃ/	
16. **j**ob	/dʒ/	/dʒ/	
17. **m**y	/m/	/m/	
18. **n**o	/n/	/n/	
19. si**ng**	/ŋ/	/ŋ/	
20. **l**et	/l/	/l/	
21. **r**ed	/r/	/r/	
22. **w**e	/w/	/w/	
23. **y**es	/y/	/y/	
24. **h**ome	/h/	/h/	

VOWEL SYMBOLS

Key Word	Well Said	Newbury	Your Dictionary
1. h**e**	/iʸ/	/ i /	
2. h**i**t	/ɪ/	/ɪ/	
3. m**ay**	/eʸ/	/eɪ/	
4. g**e**t	/ɛ/	/ɛ/	
5. m**a**d	/æ/	/æ/	
6. b**ir**d	/ɜr/	/ɜr/	
7a. c**u**p	/ʌ/	/ʌ/	
7b. **a**bout	/ə/	/ə/	
8. h**o**t, f**a**ther	/ɑ/	/ɑ/	
9. t**oo**	/uʷ/	/u/	
10. g**oo**d	/ʊ/	/ʊ/	
11. kn**ow**	/oʷ/	/oʊ/	
12. l**aw**	/ɔ/	/ɔ/	
13. f**i**ne	/aɪ/	/aɪ/	
14. n**ow**	/aʊ/	/aʊ/	
15. b**oy**	/ɔɪ/	/ɔɪ/	

Exercise 9 Look up these words in your dictionary. Write the symbol *your* dictionary uses for the boldface sound. Then check the Pronunciation Guide in your dictionary. Write the key word for the symbol.

Word	Symbol	Key Word for Symbol
Examples: in**s**urance	/ʃ/	**sh**oe
h**ea**lthy	/ɛ/	b**e**d
1. **c**omputer		
2. me**ch**anic		
3. ph**o**tographer		
4. opti**c**ian		
5. **ph**armacist		

Repeat each word after your teacher or the speaker on the audio.

You will learn more about consonant and vowel sounds and symbols in Part 2: Consonant and Vowel Supplements.

A Helpful Hint!

Keep a personal list of words that are difficult for you to say. Use the form in Appendix 1. Here are words from one student's list:

Personal Key Word List

Word	Syllables	Stress	Typical Phrase/Sentence
1. democratic	4	de mo CRA tic	a democratic government
2. asthma	2	ASTH ma /'æzmə/	an asthma attack

How do you think the dictionary helped this student with pronunciation?

Final Consonant Sounds and Linking

English words often end in consonant sounds (**car, ca<u>rd</u>, ca<u>rds</u>**). How common are final consonant sounds in your language?

In this chapter, you will learn

- The importance of final consonant sounds
  Example: lie vs. li<u>ke</u>
- The difference between final voiceless and voiced consonant sounds
  Example: grea<u>t</u> vs. *gra<u>de</u>*
- How to link final consonant sounds to the next word in a phrase
  Example: back͜up

Get Set!

1, 15 Listen to the speaker on the audio leave a telephone message. Circle the words you hear. Check your answers. Or work with a partner as follows.

Student A: Read the telephone message in the box below. Circle one word in each set of parentheses. Read the message to your partner.

Student B: Write the message. Use the form on the next page. You may ask Student A to repeat, but do not look in your partner's book until you are finished.

Message for Student A

> "This is a message for (Jay, Jake). Please tell him that (Kay, Kate) called. The meeting for new employees will be at (nine, night) in (Room A-20, Room 820). He will need to bring his new lab (coat, code)."

Form for Student B

For _____

WHILE YOU WERE OUT

_____ called

_____

Message _____

_____

_____

Signed: _____

Compare what *Student A* said and what *Student B* wrote.

Listen!

Listening Activity 1 Listen. Check a. or b.

Example: ✔ a. There's <u>J</u>oe.   ___ b. There's <u>J</u>oan.

1. ___ a. Here's the <u>tray</u>.   ___ b. Here's the <u>train</u>.

2. ___ a. Don't <u>buy</u> it.   ___ b. Don't <u>bite</u> it.

3. ___ a. Go to Gate <u>eight</u> eleven (811).   ___ b. Go to Gate <u>A</u>-11.

4. ___ a. Can you <u>dry</u>?   ___ b. Can you <u>drive</u>?

5. ___ a. The <u>cap</u> was expensive.   ___ b. The <u>cab</u> was expensive.

6. ___ a. This is my <u>right</u>.   ___ b. This is my <u>ride</u>.

Check your answers.
Now listen to both phrases. Do you hear the difference?

Rules and Practices

[1, 18] **Rule 4-1**

What happens if you omit final consonant sounds?
You might be misunderstood.

Example: *back **pain***   may sound like   *back **pay***

What you say might not make sense.

Example: ***nine*** *men*   will sound like   ***ni-*** *men*

☑ **If you want your speech to be clear, use final consonant sounds.**

[1, 19] **Rule 4-2**

What happens to the final consonant sounds in these phrases?

give up	→	gi- vup
stop it	→	sto- pit
check in	→	che- kin
drop it off	→	dro- pi- toff

☑ **Link the final consonant sound to the next word in the phrase. When the next word begins with a vowel, the final consonant sound seems to begin the next word.**

Exercise 1 Listen. Did the teacher or the speaker on the audio say the underlined sound? Check *Yes* or *No*.

	Yes	No
Examples: You're in sea<u>t</u> 8.	___ *seat 8*	✔ *C-8*
I watched them dri<u>v</u>e away.	✔ drive away	___ dry away
1. Ahmed needs some ti<u>m</u>e off.	___ time off	___ tie off
2. Did you sa<u>v</u>e anything?	___ save anything	___ say anything
3. I need to see the loa<u>n</u> officer.	___ loan officer	___ low officer
4. Kee<u>p</u> up the good work.	___ Keep up	___ Key up
5. I forgot to tie the boa<u>t</u> up.	___ boat up	___ bow up
6. What's the da<u>t</u>e of the party?	___ date of the party	___ day of the party
7. Don't bi<u>t</u>e into that.	___ bite into that	___ buy into that
8. Can the hostess sea<u>t</u> us?	___ seat us	___ see us

If you are not sure of your answers, listen again. Check your answers.

Pair Practice Take turns saying the sentences with your partner. Link the underlined sounds to the next words (e.g., *time off*).
Or, say the sentences *with* the speaker on the audio.

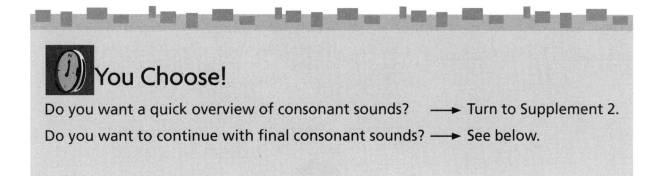

You Choose!

Do you want a quick overview of consonant sounds? ⟶ Turn to Supplement 2.

Do you want to continue with final consonant sounds? ⟶ See below.

Rule 4-3 Listen. What is the difference between the words in each pair?

A	B
ro<u>p</u>e	ro<u>b</u>e
coa<u>t</u>	co<u>d</u>e
pi<u>ck</u>	pi<u>g</u>
lea<u>f</u>	lea<u>v</u>e
pri<u>c</u>e	pri<u>z</u>e

The vowels in column B sound l-o-n-g-e-r.
Vowels are longer before voiced consonant sounds like /b/, /d/, /g/, /v/, and /z/.*

---

*The /b/, /d/, /g/, /v/, and /z/ are spoken with the voice. They are voiced consonants. The /p/, /t/ /k/, /f/, and /s/ are spoken without the voice. They are voiceless consonants.

Exercise 2

Part A Repeat the word pairs. Make the vowels in column B sound l-o-n-g-e-r.

	A *Voiceless*	*B* *Voiced*
1.	la<u>p</u>	la<u>b</u>
2.	sea<u>t</u>	see<u>d</u>
3.	coa<u>t</u>	co<u>d</u>e
4.	lo<u>ck</u>	lo<u>g</u>
5.	ba<u>ke</u>	be<u>g</u>
6.	ca<u>ke</u>	ke<u>g</u>
7.	lea<u>f</u>	lea<u>v</u>e
8.	proo<u>f</u>	pro<u>v</u>e
9.	bu<u>s</u>	bu<u>zz</u>
10.	pri<u>c</u>e	pri<u>z</u>e

Part B *Student A* says one word from a pair. *Student B* says the other word.

Example: Student A: lab. *Student B:* lap.

Cup your hands over your ears. Repeat the pair sounds like p/b, t/d, and k/g.

Notice the loud vibration when you say the second (voiced) sound in each pair. Repeat: p/b, t/d, k/g, and so on.

	Pair Sounds	*Others*
Voiceless Consonants	/ p t k f θ s ʃ tʃ /	/h/
Voiced Consonants	/ b d g v ð z ʒ dʒ /	/m n ŋ l r w y /

Exercise 3

Student A: Cover the responses. Say statement a. or b.
Student B: Cover the statements. Give the correct response. Switch roles.
Or repeat the statements and responses after the speakers on the audio.

Statements	Responses

1. a. Lo<u>ck</u> it in. **a.** Where's the key?
   b. Lo<u>g</u> it in. **b.** What's the password?

2. a. I heard about the ra<u>ce</u>. **a.** Who won?
   b. I heard about the rai<u>se</u>. **b.** How much was it?

3. a. Did she make her be<u>t</u>? **a.** No, she didn't have the money.
   b. Did she make her be<u>d</u>? **b.** No, she didn't have the time.

4. a. Should I put it in the ba<u>ck</u>? **a.** No, in the front.
   b. Should I put it in the ba<u>g</u>? **b.** No, in the box.

5. a. I forgot my lab coa<u>t</u>. **a.** You can wear mine.
   b. I forgot my lab co<u>de</u>. **b.** Just get a new number.

6. a. This a<u>che</u>* is bad. **a.** Have you seen a doctor?
   b. This e<u>gg</u> is bad. **b.** You'd better throw it away.

7. a. Take a ca<u>b</u>. **a.** It's too far to walk.
   b. Take a ca<u>p</u>. **b.** It'll keep the sun out of your eyes.

ache is pronounced /eyk/.

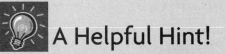

💡 A Helpful Hint!

Remember when you learned to drive a car? Or ride a bicycle? Or play a violin? You had to practice to improve. You made some mistakes but that was okay. It's the same with pronunciation. With regular practice, you'll improve. Try these strategies.

1. Practice with your **eyes closed**
2. Practice in **chorus** with your teacher and other speakers
3. Practice **silently**
4. Practice words and phrases in **slow-motion**

In the next exercise, use **silent, slow-motion** practice. You will become more aware of mouth and lip movements, especially at the ends of words.

Exercise 4 Watch your teacher deliver short messages without using her or his voice. Read the teacher's lips. Write what the teacher said. Or, work with a partner as follows.

Student A: Deliver a message without your voice. Move only your lips. Shape and **finish** each word slowly and carefully.

Student B: Read your partner's lips. Write what your partner said.

Example: Situation: One student has just gotten off the bus. She is communicating with her friend who is on the bus looking out the window.

        Speaker: See the message on page 211.

        Listener: Write the message in the bubble:

1. Situation: Two students are sitting in a noisy cafeteria. One student is communicating with his roommate on the other side of the room.

        Speaker: See the message on page 211.

        Listener: Write the message in the bubble:

2. Situation: A husband and wife are attending a dinner party. One spouse is communicating with the other across the table.

        Speaker: See the message on page 211.

        Listener: Write the message in the bubble:

        SWITCH ROLES

3. Situation: Students are sitting in a classroom listening to a lecture. One student is asking another classmate a question.

        Speaker: See the message on page 211.

        Listener: Write the message in the bubble:

4. Situation: Two friends are at a boring party on a Friday night. One friend asks the other a question.

        Speaker: See the message on page 211.

        Listener: Write the message in the bubble:

        Check your answers.

Part B Small Group Practice. Have you ever been in a similar situation? Write the situation and message below.

Situation: _____

Message: _____

In groups of four, explain your situation. Deliver the message to your group. Your group should try to lip-read the message.

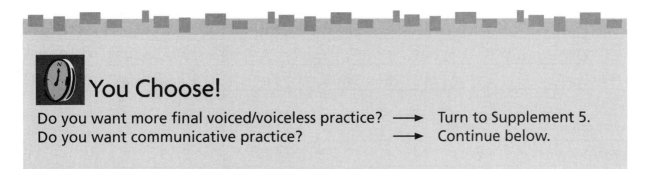

You Choose!

Do you want more final voiced/voiceless practice? ⟶ Turn to Supplement 5.
Do you want communicative practice? ⟶ Continue below.

Communicative Practice . . . survivor!

You are on a desert island. What five things do you need the most? Check five items in the chart on the next page. Write reasons for your choices. Survey three classmates and mark their choices on the chart. Was there agreement among you?

Preview: First practice the words on the next page. Include final consonants. Remember to lengthen the vowels before final voiced consonants.

Items	Votes				Reasons
	Mine	1	2	3	
coat					
sleeping bag					
cell phone					
favorite book					
pen					
lap top					
fishing rod					
knife					
fish net					
toothbrush					
sun screen					
watch					
Other:					

Pronunciation to Go! … leaving a telephone message

Practice your pronunciation in the real world. Think of a telephone message you need to leave with a friend, classmate, or co-worker in the next few days.

Step 1: Who is the message for? _____

What will you say? _____

_____

_____

_____

Step 2: Underline the final sounds. Link ⌣ final sounds to the next word in the phrase.

Step 3: Practice the message several times before you leave it.

Step 4: Leave the message.

Syllables and *-s* Endings

The *-s* ending is common in English.

In this chapter, you will learn about the importance of -s endings.

You will also learn . . .

tap   *tap - tap*

- When the *-s* ending is an extra syllable: teach ⟶ teach - es

tap   *tap*

- When the *-s* ending is just an added sound: book ⟶ books

Get Set!

Pair Practice Look at the business cards. Write one or two things that each person *does.*

Example:

Maria takes pictures at weddings. She also makes videos.

1. _____   2. _____

3. _____   4. _____

Dictate your answers to your teacher. Or write your answers on the board. With your class, find all of the words that need *-s* endings.

Listen!

Listening Activity 1 Listen to the teacher or the speaker on the audio say phrase a. or phrase b. Circle the one that you hear.

Examples: He   a. works day and night.
          They   (b.) work day and night.

          She   (a.) runs errands.
          They   b. run errands.

1. He   a. plays music.
   They b. play music.

2. She   a. grades papers.
   They b. grade papers.

3. She   a. takes pictures at weddings.
   They b. take pictures at weddings.

4. She   a. fixes cars.
   They b. fix cars.

5. She   a. teaches English.
   They b. teach English.

Check your answers.
Now listen to both phrases in each pair.

Listening Activity 2 Listen to your teacher or the speaker on the audio say one of the sentences in each of the following pairs. Circle the one you hear.

Example: Could you feed my (cat)?   Could you feed my (cats)?

1. He left his business (card).   He left his business (cards).

2. Ari works with his (cousin).   Ari works with his (cousins).

3. When did your (guest) arrive?   When did your (guests) arrive?

4. Let me wash the (dish).   Let me wash the (dishes).

5. Who sent the (rose)?   Who sent the (roses)?

6. I didn't get your (message).   I didn't get your (messages).

7. Put the (fax) on my desk.   Put the (faxes) on my desk.

Check your answers.
Listen to both sentences in each pair.

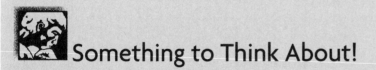

Something to Think About!

What happens when you omit *-s* endings?

- Sometimes the meaning is not clear.

  Example: John hit a tree and broke his leg(s).

- Sometimes the meaning is clear, but the listener might be bothered or distracted.

  Example: All my teacher(s) alway(s) give quiz(zes) on Friday(s).

Rules and Practices

We use -s endings for the following:

PRESENT TENSE: Dr. Patel teach**es** at 10:00.   (third person, singular)
PLURALS: Liz takes care of pet**s**.
POSSESSIVES: Lee**'s** keys are in the car.
CONTRACTIONS: He**'s** back.

Rule 5-1

We pronounce -s endings three ways. Listen to the final -s in each group.
Do you hear /s/, /z/, or /əz/? Circle what you hear.

				Circle		
Group 1:	pet**s**,	sleep**s**,	Mike's ⟶	/s/	/z/	/əz/
Group 2:	dog**s**,	drive**s**,	Lee's ⟶	/s/	/z/	/əz/
Group 3:	fax**es**,	teach**es**,	Rose's ⟶	/s/	/z/	/əz/

☑ **Compare your answers with these rules:**

Group 1:   If the word ends in a voiceless sound (pe<u>t</u>, slee<u>p</u>, Mi<u>k</u>e), add the voiceless hissing sound /s/.

Group 2:   If the word ends in a voiced sound (do<u>g</u>, dri<u>v</u>e, L<u>ee</u>), add the voiced buzzing sound /z/.

Group 3:   If the word already ends in a hissing or buzzing sound (fa<u>x</u>, tea<u>ch</u>, Ro<u>se</u>), add the syllable /əz/ or /ɪz/.

Note: Contractions with is *or* has *follow the same rules:*

What**'s** her name?   He**'s** been to Europe.   Rose**'s** sick.
/s/   /z/   /əz/

Exercise 1 Repeat these words after your teacher or the speaker on the audio.

ADD A SOUND		ADD A SYLLABLE
/s/	/z/	/əz/ or /ɪz/
likes	needs	houses
tapes	rides	dishes
weeks	songs	watches
coats	keys	closes
laughs	phones	messages
drinks	wears	practices
Jack's slacks	Lee's keys	Jess's dresses
Burt's shirts	Bob's jobs	Liz's quizzes
Mike's bikes	Lou's shoes	Cass's glasses
_____	_____	_____
_____	_____	_____
_____	_____	_____

With your partner, add each word to the correct list above.

taxes
hot dogs
quits
offices
locks
bosses
bills
miles
works

Check your answers.

Rule 5-2 Don't let the *-es* spelling confuse you.

Sometimes *e* in *-es* is silent.

tap	→	*tap*	
love		loves	(sounds like /lʌvz/)
hope		hopes	(sounds like /hoʷps/)

Sometimes *-es* is a syllable.

tap	→	*tap – tap*	
nurse		nurs - es	(sounds like *nurse is*)

☑ **The *–es* sounds like the syllable /əz/ or the word *is* /ɪz/ after hissing or buzzing sounds: /s, z, ʃ, ʒ, tʃ, dʒ /.** *Example:* hou<u>s</u>es = *house is*; mat<u>ch</u>es = *match is*; pa<u>g</u>es = *page is.*

Exercise 2 Repeat the words and sentences after your teacher or the speaker on the audio. Tap a pen or pencil as you say each word.

tap → *tap*

1. love	loves	Lizzie **loves** animals.
2. write	writes	Naomi **writes** poetry.
3. name	names	Our teacher has finally learned our **names**.
4. think	thinks	Marty **thinks** about his girlfriend all the time.
5. eat	eats	Dr. Patel **eats** lunch at her desk.

tap → *tap – tap*

6. wash	wash - es	Amin **washes** his car on Sundays.
7. price	pric - es	Which store has the best **prices**?
8. bridge	bridg - es	Cross two **bridges** and then turn right.
9. box	box - es	We need two **boxes** of cereal.
10. miss	miss - es	George never **misses** class.

Exercise 3 Repeat each sentence twice—once in the singular and once in the plural. Or, work with a partner as follows.

Student A: Circle one of the words in each set of parentheses. Say each sentence with the word you have chosen.

Student B: Listen to Student A. Circle ☝ for singular. Circle ✌ for plural. Do not look in your partner's book.

Student A

Examples: Which (suitcase, suitcases) did you take?

Do the (exercise, exercises) for homework.

1. Henry broke our new (glass, glasses).
2. I paid for the (ticket, tickets).
3. Which (language, languages) did you study in school?
4. Pay the cashier for your (purchase, purchases).
5. Did you listen to your (message, messages)?

6. His (wish, wishes) came true. ☝ ✌

7. My most interesting (class is, classes are) in the morning. ☝ ✌

8. The law (office is, offices are) around the corner. ☝ ✌

9. The dirty (dish is, dishes are) in the sink. ☝ ✌

10. I didn't study for the (quiz, quizzes). ☝ ✌

Check your answers with your partner. Switch roles and repeat the activity.

A Helpful Hint!

Do your want your speech to sound smooth and natural?
Link the *-s* ending to the next word in the phrase:

     gets up   Zia get**s** up at 5:00 A.M.   (sounds like *get sup*)

When the final *-s* sound links to the same or a similar sound, it seems to get lost.

     gets sick   Javier never get**s** sick.   (sounds like *get sick*)

Exercise 4 Look at the underlined endings. Write how to say them—/s/, /z/, or /əz/. Check your answers. Then ask your classmates about their habits.

Find a person who *often* does the following:

Example: _____Sam_____ often cook<u>s</u> at home.

                                     /s/

1. _____ often sleep<u>s</u> past noon.

2. _____ ride<u>s</u> a bike to school or work.

3. _____ often los<u>es</u> things.

4. _____ sing<u>s</u> in the shower.

5. _____ often eat<u>s</u> dessert.

Find a person who *never* does the following:

6. _____ never drink<u>s</u> coffee.

7. _____ never get<u>s</u> angry.

8. _____ never miss<u>es</u> class.

9. _____ never us<u>es</u> e-mail.

10. _____ never sleep<u>s</u> late—past six A.M.

Now share your answers with the class. Link the *-s* endings.

★ Prime-Time Practice

Prime-time practice is speaking homework that you do between the prime-time hours of 7:00 P.M. and 11:00 P.M.

Step 1: Close your book and listen to "Odd Jobs." Listen again and fill in the blanks.

ODD JOBS

Do you work to live or live to work? The answer probably depends on your job. These five people love their _____. Do any of these jobs appeal to you?

- Cindy _____ in a potato chip factory. If she sees _____ that are overcooked, she removes them—or eats them!

- Louis is a page turner. He turns _____ of music for pianists when they play in New York City.

- Brian tests video games. He _____ games eight hours a day, five _____ a week, and he never gets bored.

- Jeff dives for golf _____ in lakes in Florida. Every week he finds about 25,000 balls and _____ them for five to ten cents each.

- John is a taste tester. He _____ ice cream four to five hours a day and _____ paid to do it!

Step 2: Check the Answer Key. Notice that almost 25 percent of the words have *-s* endings!

Step 3: Read "Odd Jobs" *with* the speaker at least three times.

Step 4: Record yourself reading "Odd Jobs." Listen to your recording.

a. I pronounced the *-s* ending in these words:

_____   _____   _____   _____

b. I omitted the *-s* ending in these words:

_____   _____   _____   _____

Communicative Practice . . . discussing routine job activities

Imagine that you have your ideal job right now. What is it? What do you do every day?

Step 1: Create a business card that shows what you do.

Step 2: Describe your business card to your partner. Describe the work that you do. Listen to your partner describe his or her business card to you. Take notes here.

_____

_____

_____

Step 3: Describe your partner's dream job to a small group or to the class. Tell the class what your partner does.

Syllables and *-ed* Endings

The *-ed* ending is common in English.

> Carlos need**ed** to study.
> Kim mov**ed** out last weekend.

In this chapter you will learn about the importance of *-ed* endings.

You will also learn . . .

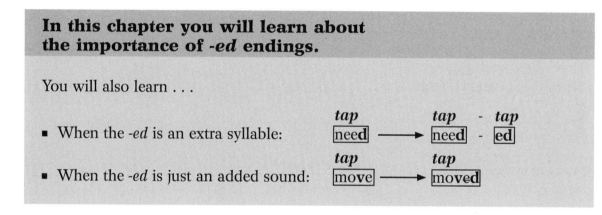

- When the *-ed* is an extra syllable:

tap		*tap*	-	*tap*
need	→	need	-	ed

- When the *-ed* is just an added sound:

tap		*tap*
move	→	mov**ed**

Get Set!

Your friend has called to tell you about his date. He is talking on his cell phone. Some words are not clear. Guess the missing words.

 1, 37 Now listen to your teacher or the speaker on the audio read the message. Fill in the blanks with the words you hear.

"It was a disaster! First, I got lost and _____ her up an hour late. We finally got to the restaurant, and everything was going pretty well until I _____ eating my steak, and she told me she was a vegetarian. Then, I paid the server, and I _____ a glass of water onto her shoe. She _____ herself and went to the restroom – and she never _____!"

How many of your answers end in *-ed*? ____ Compare your answers with your partner's. Dictate your answers to your teacher or write them on the board.

Missing words: picked, started, knocked, excused, returned.

Listen!

Listening Activity 1 Present or Past? Listen. Circle a. or b.

Example: (a.) We **want** to eat out.
     b. We **wanted** to eat out.

1. a. They always **arrive** on time.
   b. They always **arrived** on time.

2. a. The restaurants **close** at 11:00 on Saturday.
   b. The restaurants **closed** at 11:00 on Saturday.

3. a. The servers **add** a tip to the check.
   b. The servers **added** a tip to the check.

4. a. They often **walk** home.
   b. They often **walked** home.

5. a. She **needs** to go to the bank.
   b. She **needed** to go to the bank.

Check your answers.

Listen again.

Then listen to both a. and b.

Listening Activity 2 Listen to the teacher or the speaker on the audio say the words. Write the number of syllables.

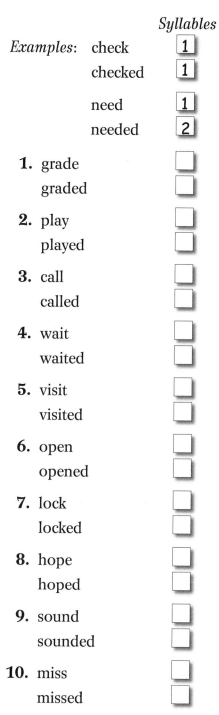

		Syllables
Examples:	check	1
	checked	1
	need	1
	needed	2
1.	grade	
	graded	
2.	play	
	played	
3.	call	
	called	
4.	wait	
	waited	
5.	visit	
	visited	
6.	open	
	opened	
7.	lock	
	locked	
8.	hope	
	hoped	
9.	sound	
	sounded	
10.	miss	
	missed	

Check your answers.
Listen again.

Rules and Practices

Rule 6-1

(1, 43)

We pronounce final -*ed* three ways. Listen to -*ed* in each group.
Do you hear /t/, /d/, or /ɪd/? Circle the sound you hear.

Circle

Group 1:	needed,	rested,	started	⟶	/t/	/d/	/ɪd/
Group 2:	planned,	moved,	called	⟶	/t/	/d/	/ɪd/
Group 3:	picked,	missed,	thanked	⟶	/t/	/d/	/ɪd/

☑ **Compare your answers with these rules:**

Group 1: When the last sound is /d/ or /t/ (nee**d**, res**t**), add the syllable /ɪd/ or /əd/.
Example: nee**d**-ed

Group 2: When the last sound is voiced (pla**n**, mo**v**e), add /d/.
Example: pla**nn**ed/plænd/

Group 3: When the last sound is voiceless (pi**ck**, mi**ss**), add /t/.
Example: pi**ck**ed /pɪkt/

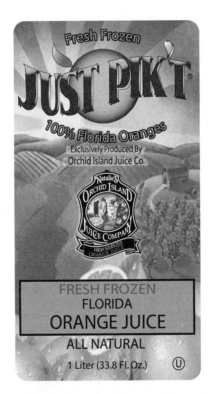

▲ **Figure 6-2** This label shows *picked* as it is spoken.

Exercise 1 Repeat these words after your teacher or the speaker on the audio.

ADD A SOUND		ADD A SYLLABLE
/t/	/d/	/ɪd/ or /ed/
washed	used	waited
laughed	moved	needed
asked	caused	added
worked	closed	wanted
passed	opened	decided
stopped	applied	estimated
finished	required	graduated
_____	_____	_____
_____	_____	_____

Say these words. Write them in the correct box above.

changed
stayed
missed
planted
looked
painted

Check your answers.

Choose two words from the box above. Write a sentence with each word. Practice saying the sentences.

1. _____

2. _____

Dictate the sentences to your partner. Write your partner's sentences here.

1. _____

2. _____

Check your sentences.

Exercise 2 Homonyms are *spelled differently* but *pronounced the same.*
Example: road = rowed

Find homonyms for these words in the Word Search Box. Circle them. The first one (*guest = guessed*) is done for you. The rest of the homonyms are *-ed* verbs like *guessed*.

guest	least
past	disgust
find	mind
pact	mist

Word Search Box

d	e	u	e	a	p	f	m
i	c	e	l	g	a	i	i
s	k	d	e	u	c	n	s
c	a	e	a	e	k	e	s
u	p	a	s	s	e	d	e
s	g	n	e	s	d	i	d
s	s	s	d	e	i	d	g
e	e	m	e	d	e	s	u
d	m	i	n	e	d	e	i

Check your answers.

Something to Think About!

For natural speech, link the *-ed* sound to the next word in the phrase. When the next word starts with a vowel sound, the *-ed* ending will be clear and easy to hear.

Example: They live**d** in Cairo   *sounds like*   They live **d**in Cairo.

When the next word starts with a consonant sound, the *-ed* ending might be hard to hear, especially if the next sound is the same or similar.

Example: They live**d** downtown   *sounds like*   They live downtown.
Example: They live**d** three blocks away   *sounds like*   They live three blocks away.

Practice linking in the next exercise.

Exercise 3 *Student A:* Say sentence a. or b. *Student B:* Mark *Now* or *Then*.

(1, 45) Or, listen to the speaker say a. or b. Mark *Now* or *Then*.

Example: a. We use a credit card for our groceries.   Now ✔
                b. We used a credit card for our groceries.   Then ☐

1. a. I like *Animal Farm.*   Now ☐
    b. I liked *Animal Farm.*   Then ☐

2. a. We play computer games.   Now ☐
    b. We played computer games.   Then ☐

3. a. I cook dinner every night.   Now ☐
    b. I cooked dinner every night.   Then ☐

4. a. I walk almost everywhere.   Now ☐
    b. I walked almost everywhere.   Then ☐

5. a. We listen to the Beatles.   Now ☐
    b. We listened to the Beatles.   Then ☐

6. a. I study every night.   Now ☐
    b. I studied every night.   Then ☐

7. a. I play soccer every weekend.   Now ☐
    b. I played soccer every weekend.   Then ☐

8. a. She sounds upset.   Now ☐
    b. She sounded upset.   Then ☐

(1, 46) Check your answers. Which *-ed* endings were easy to hear? Which were difficult?

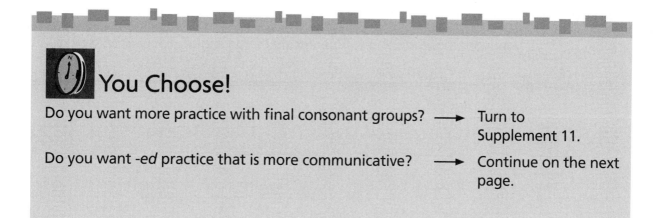

You Choose!

Do you want more practice with final consonant groups?   ⟶   Turn to Supplement 11.

Do you want *-ed* practice that is more communicative?   ⟶   Continue on the next page.

Exercise 4 Reader's Theater

Step 1: Listen to the fable. Then read along *with* the teacher or the speakers on the audio as many times as you wish.

Step 2: In groups of four, choose a role. Practice reading the fable with your group. Pay attention to all final sounds, but especially final *-s* and *-ed*. Take turns reading each role.

Step 3 (Optional): Take turns performing for the class.

The Old Man and His Sons

Readers:	Reader 1	Reader 2	Reader 3	The Farmer

Reader 1: Welcome to this presentation of a fable by Aesop call**ed** "The Old Man and His Son**s**."

Reader 2: Once there was a poor farmer who work**ed** very hard. He had many son**s**.

Reader 3: His son**s** argu**ed** all the time.

Reader 1: One day the farmer ask**ed** his son**s** to come inside the house.

Reader 2: He hand**ed** each son a bundle of stick**s** and said . . .

Farmer: I want each of you to break this bundle of stick**s** in two.

Reader 3: Each son tri**ed** but he fail**ed**.

Reader 1: The farmer smil**ed**. Then he hand**ed** each son one stick from the bundle and said . . .

Farmer: I want each of you to try to break just one stick.

Reader 2: Of course, each son could easily break one stick. The farmer said . . .

Farmer: I hope you have learn**ed** a lesson from this bundle of stick**s**.

All: If you work together, you will be strong. If you argue, you will be weak.

Exercise 5 TOEFL® iBT Speaking Practice (Optional)

Describe one of the best teachers you have ever had and explain why this person was a good teacher. Include details to support your explanation.

Take 15 seconds to prepare and 45 seconds to respond. Record your answer. Listen to your recording. Are your -s and -ed endings clear?

⭐ Prime-Time Practice

Campus Slang and Idioms

The TOEFL now includes slang and idioms. Many of these expressions end in -ed.

Step 1: Match the underlined word/phrase with the definition. Check the Answer Key.

1. ____ Ari doesn't drink. He offered to be our <u>designated driver</u>.

    a. got a grade of A

2. ____ I <u>flunked</u> my math midterm.

    b. person who does not drink alcohol and drives friends home

3. ____ I <u>aced</u> my biology final.

    c. excited

4. ____ My parents <u>freaked out</u> when they heard about my car wreck.

    d. got a grade of F

5. ____ I wasn't hurt, but my car was <u>totaled</u>.

    e. lost control

6. ____ Maria is totally <u>psyched</u> about her ski trip.

    f. so badly damaged it could not be repaired

Step 2: Decide how to pronounce the -ed words. Check the Answer Key. Practice the sentences. Remember to link -ed, especially in sentences 1, 4, and 6.

Step 3: Record yourself saying the sentences. Listen to your recording.
I omitted -ed in these words:

_____ _____ _____ _____ _____

I pronounced -ed in these words:

_____ _____ _____ _____ _____

🎧 You may listen to the speaker on the audio read the sentences at any time.

1, 48

Communicative Practice ... timelines

What were four or five important events in your life?

For each event, write the year on a line below. Write what happened next to the year.

These verbs might be useful:

realized	finished	accepted	passed
applied	moved	got hired	returned
got accepted	immigrated	got promoted	was introduced
graduated	visited	learned	got married
started	got offered	joined	got divorced

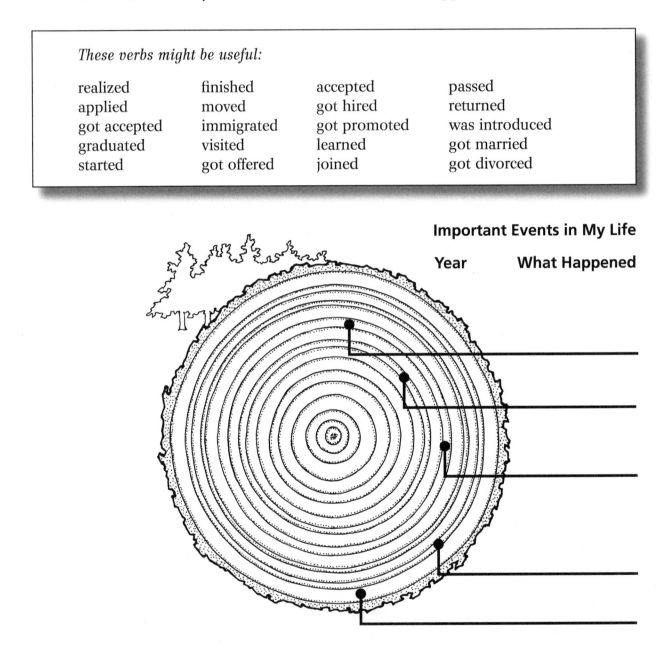

Important Events in My Life

Year   **What Happened**

Share one or two events with your partner or small group. Ask and answer questions about these events.

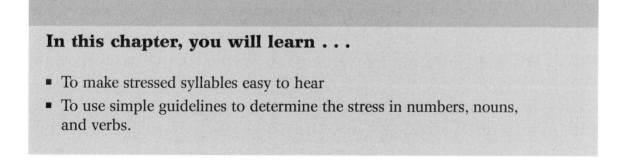

Stressed Syllables—
Numbers, Nouns, and Verbs

In words with two or more syllables, one syllable is stronger than the others. This syllable has the most stress.

In this chapter, you will learn . . .

- To make stressed syllables easy to hear
- To use simple guidelines to determine the stress in numbers, nouns, and verbs.

Get Set!

Listen to the dialogue. Circle the words you hear. Check your answers. Or, work with a partner as follows.

Student A: Choose a word in each set of parentheses below. Tell your partner about your busy morning. *Student B:* Choose responses that make sense.

Branching Dialogue

A: First, I returned Robert's book on Southwestern (desserts, deserts).

B: Oh, do you like to cook?   B: Oh, do you like geography?

A: I do. Then I finally got that (massage, message) from Ivan I've been waiting for.

B: That sounds relaxing.   B: I hope it was good news.

A: It was! After that, Jenny and I discussed the (comedy, committee).

B: Did she think it was funny?   B: Did she think we need more members?

A: She did. By then, everyone in the department was hungry, so I ordered pizza for (nineteen, ninety).

B: About 20. That's a small department.   B: Almost 100. That's a big department!

Now check your answers with your partner.
Which words caused confusion? Discuss them with your class.

Listen!

 Listening Activity 1 Listen to the teacher or the speaker on the audio say one word in each pair. Check the word you hear.

Example: ___ thirty ✓ thirteen

1. ___ tulips   ___ two lips
2. ___ message   ___ massage
3. ___ often   ___ offend
4. ___ personal   ___ personnel
5. ___ element   ___ a limit
6. ___ common   ___ come on
7. ___ object (*noun*)   ___ object (*verb*)
8. ___ eleven   ___ elephant

Check your answers.

Now listen to both words in each pair.

Something to Think About!

When word stress is wrong, your listener might not understand you—even if all your sounds are correct!

If you stress the *wrong* syllable,
dessert   might sound like   *desert*

If you stress *all* syllables,
specialty   might sound like   *special tea*

Listening Activity 2 Listen for the strong syllable.

Part A You will hear *DA-də* (STRONG-weak) or *də-DA* (weak-STRONG).
Check the one you hear.

	$\overline{\text{DA}}$-də	də-$\overline{\text{DA}}$
Examples:	✔	
		✔
1.		
2.		
3.		
4.		
5.		

Check your answers.

Part B Listen to the words. Do they sound like *DA-də* or *də-DA*?

	$\overline{\text{DA}}$-də	də-$\overline{\text{DA}}$
Examples: promise	✔	
result		✔
1. succeed		
2. famous		
3. present, n.		
4. present, v.		
5. record, n.		
6. record, v.		
7. enjoy		
8. method		
9. today		
10. sister		

Check your answers.

Rules and Practices

In English, it is difficult to know which syllable to stress. These guidelines will help, but there will be exceptions. When you learn new words, learn the stress patterns too!

Rule 7-1

Listen to the numbers. Notice the stress patterns.

    FORty   fourTEEN
    EIGHty   eighTEEN

☑ **The *-teen* numbers are usually stressed on the -TEEN syllable when they come at the end of a phrase or sentence.**

Exercise 1 *Student A*: Circle a. or b. Say the sentence. *Student B*: Check (✓) the sentence you hear.

STUDENT A	**STUDENT B**

Examples: a. Class begins at 4:15. ☐
 b. Class begins at 4:50. ✓

1. a. I'd like to make a reservation for 18. ☐
 b. I'd like to make a reservation for 80. ☐

2. a. That'll be $4.16. ☐
 b. That'll be $4.60. ☐

3. a. I live at eight ninety (890) Green Street. ☐
 b. I live at eight nineteen (819) Green Street. ☐

4. a. Our party's on the thirteenth. ☐
 b. Our party's on the thirtieth. ☐

5. a. Get off at Exit 14. ☐
 b. Get off at Exit 40. ☐

SWITCH ROLES

6. a. The movie starts at 7:15. ☐
 b. The movie starts at 7:50. ☐

7. a. Your flight to Seoul leaves from Gate 14. ☐
 b. Your flight to Seoul leaves from Gate 40. ☐

8. a. She's 17. ☐
 b. She's 70. ☐

9. a. The room is 12 by 13. ☐
 b. The room is 12 by 30. ☐

10. a. Take bus number 16. ☐
 b. Take bus number 60. ☐

Check your answers.
Listen to both a. and b. Repeat.

2, 7

Note: English speakers usually stress the first syllable when counting -teen numbers: THIRteen, FOURteen, FIFteen, etc.

Rule 7-2

Listen to these two-syllable nouns. Notice the stress pattern.

COUNtry
DOCtor
PENcil

☑ **Stress the first syllable. About 90 percent of all two-syllable nouns have first-syllable stress.**

Rule 7-3

Listen to these two-syllable verbs. Notice the stress pattern.

enJOY
disCUSS
subTRACT

☑ **Stress the second syllable. About 60 percent of all two-syllable verbs have second-syllable stress.**

Exercise 2 Say these words *with* your teacher or the speaker on the audio. Raise your hand as you say the stressed syllable. Imagine that you are lifting a heavy weight.

2-SYLLABLE NOUNS	2-SYLLABLE VERBS
actor	agree
dentist	debate
student	occur
mother	complain
jacket	advise
music	protect
problem	employ
reason	behave

Write five two-syllable nouns and five two-syllable verbs. Look them up in your dictionary. Mark the syllable with primary stress.

_____   _____

_____   _____

_____   _____

_____   _____

_____   _____

Do these words follow Rules 7-2 and 7-3? Remember: you will find more exceptions for verbs than for nouns!

Rule 7-4

Listen to the noun-verb pairs. Notice the stress patterns.

Noun: the PROduce   Jean went to the market for fresh PROduce.
Verb: to proDUCE   How much oil does Venezuela proDUCE?

Noun: a REcord   Al keeps a REcord of what he spends.
Verb: to reCORD   Can we reCORD the lecture?

☑ **Stress the first syllable when the word is a noun. Stress the second syllable when the word is a verb.**

Exercise 3 Say the word pairs *with* the teacher or the speaker on the audio.

Noun	Verb
CONduct	conDUCT
CONtract	conTRACT
DESert	deSERT
OBject	obJECT
PERmit	perMIT
PREsent	preSENT
PROduce	proDUCE
PROgress	proGRESS
PROject	proJECT
REcord	reCORD
REfuse	reFUSE
SUSpect	susPECT

Repeat the exercise. If *Student A* says the noun, *Student B* says the verb and vice versa.

Example: Student A says . . . CONduct
          Student B says . . . conDUCT

Note: Not all *two-syllable noun-verb pairs change stress: an ANswer /to ANswer; a deLAY/to deLAY; a rePORT/to rePORT; a PROmise /to PROmise; a rePLY /to rePLY.*

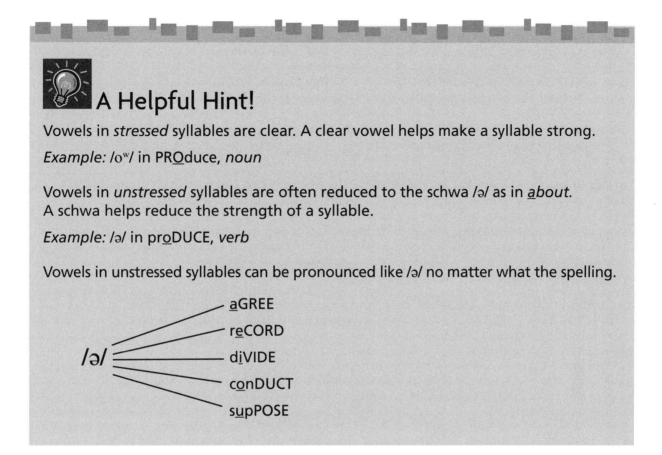

A Helpful Hint!

Vowels in *stressed* syllables are clear. A clear vowel helps make a syllable strong.

Example: /oʷ/ in PROduce, *noun*

Vowels in *unstressed* syllables are often reduced to the schwa /ə/ as in *about*. A schwa helps reduce the strength of a syllable.

Example: /ə/ in proDUCE, *verb*

Vowels in unstressed syllables can be pronounced like /ə/ no matter what the spelling.

/ə/ —— aGREE
/ə/ —— reCORD
/ə/ —— diVIDE
/ə/ —— conDUCT
/ə/ —— supPOSE

Exercise 4 With your partner, circle the correct form. Take turns saying each sentence.

Example: Which countries (PROduce, (proDUCE)) the most oil?

1. Did you remember to get some (PROduce, proDUCE)?

2. We finally finished the (SURvey, surVEY).

3. Have you made any (PROgress, proGRESS)?

4. Does anyone (OBject, obJECT)?

5. This button lets you (REcord, reCORD) your messages.

6. Take this form to student (REcords, reCORDS).

7. I have a question about the final (PROject, proJECT).

8. You can (PREsent, preSENT) your ideas at the next meeting.

9. Did you sign the (CONtract, conTRACT)?

10. She made an offer I couldn't (REfuse, reFUSE).

Now listen and repeat.

Rule 7-5*

[2, 14]

Listen to these noun-phrasal verb pairs. Notice the stress patterns.

Noun	a CHECKout	There's a long line at the CHECKout.
Phrasal Verb	to check OUT	Are you ready to check OUT?
Noun	a TAKEoff	That was a smooth TAKEoff.
Phrasal Verb	to take OFF	Don't take OFF without saying goodbye.

☑ **Stress is on the first part of the noun and the second part of the phrasal verb.***

Exercise 5 *Student A says a. or b. Student B says the matching sentence.*

Student A	**Student B**
1. a. BREAKup	Tom was sad about his BREAKup with Megan.
b. break UP	They had a disagreement and decided to break UP.
2. a. TAKEout	Let's not cook tonight. Let's get TAKEout.
b. take OUT	I asked them to pack it to take OUT.
3. a. LAYoff	There were twenty LAYoffs last month.
b. lay OFF	How many workers are they going to lay OFF?
4. a. HANDout	The homework is on the HANDout.
b. hand OUT	Would you mind handing these OUT?
5. a. PICKup	She drives a small PICKup.
b. pick UP	When should I pick you UP?

[2, 15]

Switch roles.
Listen to the phrases and sentences. Repeat.

Note these exceptions: HAND the PApers out; I PICKED JOHN up. When a direct object noun is used with a phrasal verb, stress is usually on the first part of the phrasal verb and the direct object.

⭐ Prime-Time Practice

More Campus Slang and Idioms

The TOEFL now includes slang and idioms like these noun/phrasal-verb pairs:

Noun: a HANGout
Verb: to hang OUT

Step 1: Read the paragraph. Write the underlined word/phrase next to the definition. Check the Answer Key.

MY WEEKEND

My roommates and I had a quiet weekend. On Friday night, we didn't want to

<u>shell out</u>¹ a bunch of money for a movie so we just <u>hung out</u>² in the room and talked.

Ten bucks for a movie is kind of a <u>ripoff</u>³ anyway. On Saturday and Sunday, we studied

Too much

all day. We'd missed some classes during the week and had to <u>catch up</u>⁴. Then on

Sunday night, we ordered a few pizzas, got a gallon of ice cream and <u>pigged out</u>⁵.

- spent time with friends   _____
- pay   _____
- ate a lot of food at one time   _____
- something that costs more than it is worth _____
- complete late or missed work   _____

Step 2: Mark the stress in the underlined phrases. Check the Answer Key. Practice the phrases. Remember to link (e.g., shell out, rip off, pigged out, etc.).

Step 3: Record yourself reading the paragraph. Listen to the recording.

Step 4: Monitor the underlined words.

I used the correct stress in these words:

_____ _____ _____ _____

I need to improve my stress in these words:

_____ _____ _____ _____

Listen to the speaker on the audio read the paragraph at any time.

2, 16

Rule 7-6

Listen to these compound nouns. Notice the main stress.

> CLASSroom
> MAILbox
> FLASHlight

☑ **The main stress is on the first word or first part of the compound noun.**

Sometimes the compound is written as two words: CELL phone, HEALTH center, STOCK market, BAR code. It is still pronounced like one word with one main stress.

Exercise 6 Say these compound nouns *with* your teacher or the speaker on the audio.

Add movement to your practice. As you say the stressed syllable, raise your arm. Or tap your hand. Or tap your pencil. Or stretch a rubber band.

Examples: SIDEwalk
STOPsign
HIGHway

GOLFball	PASSword	SHOEstore	POPcorn
BASEball	VOICEmail	BOOKstore	BIRTHday
SUNroof	HOMEwork	RESTroom	PANcakes
KEYring	WEBsite	BEDroom	CHEESEcake
EARring	COFfee mug	DISHwasher	TALK show

Can you think of more compound nouns? _____ _____ _____

Communicative Practice ... travel game

You are taking a trip to Barcelona by plane. Here is a list of items to pack in your carry-on luggage. First practice saying the items on the list.

List

RAINcoat	WASH cloth
TOOTHpaste	CANdy bar
TOOTHbrush	BEACH towel
GUIDEbook	SUNscreen
PHRASEbook	CELL phone
PASSport	EARplugs
NOTEbook	SWEATshirt
LAPtop	SWEATpants
SUITcoat	MAKEup
BATH soap	FLASHlight

In groups of four to six, play this game.

Example: *Student A:* I went on a trip to ____, and I took a <u>LAPtop</u>.
              Student B: I went on a trip to ____, and I took a <u>LAPtop</u> and <u>PASSport</u>.
              Student C: I went on a trip to ____, and I took a <u>LAPtop</u>, <u>PASSport</u>, and <u>PHRASEbook</u>.

Players continue until they forget an item. Pay close attention to stress patterns.

Pronunciation to Go!

Apply your pronunciation skills to everyday interactions.

Task: Order at the snack bar the next time you go to a movie theater.

Pronunciation Point: Stress in Compound Nouns

Before: Practice useful words and phrases.

All candy............1.50   Hot Dogs.....3.00
Popcorn   Small.....2.00
          Medium...3.00   Ice Cream...2.50
          Large.....3.50
Drinks   Small.....2.00   Snacks......2.00
          Medium...2.50   (peanuts, cracker
          Large.....3.00   jacks)

Sample Practice Dialogue:

A: I'd like a BUTerfinger and a medium POPcorn.
B: That'll be four FIFty.
A: Here you go.
B: No. Four FIFty, not four fifTEEN.
A: Oh, sorry.

Key Vocabulary

MOvie theatre
SNACK bar
HOT dog
POPcorn
PEAnuts
ICE cream
SOFT drinks
CANdy bars
BUTterfinger
MILK duds
PEAnut butter cups
CRAcker jacks

After: Report your experience to the class.

Stressed Syllables—Suffixes

Suffixes are syllables added to the end of a word:

-ic   as in   hero<u>ic</u>
-ity   as in   abil<u>ity</u>
-ion as in   educat<u>ion</u>

In this chapter, you will learn . . .

- To predict stressed syllables in words with common suffixes.
- To make stressed syllables *l-o-n-g* and **clear.**

Get Set!

The way you sleep could tell something about your personality, according to a study. Find your favorite sleep position. Write the number below. Then read about your personality type.

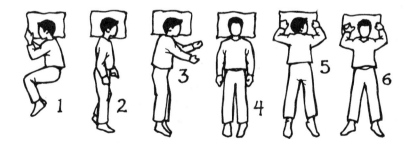

My favorite sleeping position is number _____.

1. You are tough on the outside but have a lot of **sensitivity** on the inside. You are shy and have feelings of **inferiority** when you first meet someone but soon relax.

2. You are known for your friendliness and **sociability.** You enjoy **popularity** and being part of the in-crowd. Although you are trusting, sometimes you are too trusting.

3. You are known for your openness and **sincerity,** but you can be suspicious and **cynical** too. You are **practical** and slow to make **decisions.**

4. You are reserved and quiet. You seek **serenity.** You also seek **perfection** and set high standards for yourself and others.

5. You are known for your friendliness and **hospitality,** but those qualities may hide a nervous **personality.** You are sometimes self-centered and **egotistical.**

6. You are a good friend and listener. You are known for your **generosity.** You do not like to be the center of **attention.**

These qualities apply to me: These qualities do not apply to me:

_____   _____

_____   _____

_____   _____

Look at the qualities you listed, especially the ones that are boldface. Circle the syllables that you think have the main stress.

Does your sleep position describe you? Tell the members in your group why or why not.

Listen!

Listening Activity 1 Listen to the teacher or speaker on the audio say each word two times. Circle the strongest syllable.

Example: per-so- na-li-ty

1. po-si-tion
2. at-ten-tion
3. sin-ce-ri-ty
4. de-ci-sion
5. po-pu-la-ri-ty
6. ge-ne-ro-si-ty
7. per-fec-tion
8. sen-si-ti-vi-ty

Check your answers.
Listen again.

A Helpful Hint!

What makes a stressed syllable sound strong?

The vowel in the stressed syllable is clear.   a-GREE-ment

The stressed syllable is higher in pitch.   a-^GREE^-ment

The vowel is long and stretched out.   a-**GRE E**-ment

Listening Activity 2 Listen to the teacher or speaker on the audio say these words. Which syllable is the *clearest* and *longest*? Check 1st (NA-tion-al), 2nd (per-FEC-tion), or 3rd (gua-ran-TEE). Number one is done for you.

	1st ____ . . NA-tion-al	2nd . ____ . per-FEC-tion	3rd . . ____ gua-ran-TEE
1. e-lec-tric		✔	
2. am-bi-tion			
3. Ja-pa-nese			
4. en-gin-eer			
5. pos-si-ble			
6. de-ve-lop			
7. fan-tas-tic			
8. prac-ti-cal			
9. beau-ti-ful			
10. un-der-stand			

Check your answers.
Now listen to the words in the three columns.

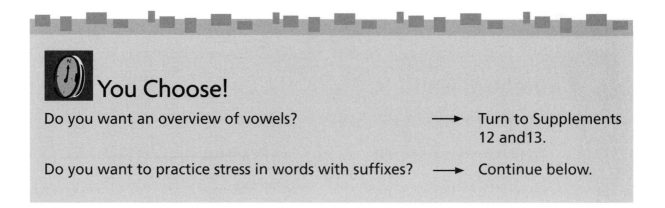

You Choose!

Do you want an overview of vowels?   ⟶   Turn to Supplements 12 and13.

Do you want to practice stress in words with suffixes?   ⟶   Continue below.

Rules and Practices

Many common suffixes *do not* change word stress. Listen.

-ness	HAPpy	HAPp<u>iness</u>
-ful	BEAUty	BEAUt<u>iful</u>
-ment	reQUIRE	reQUIRE<u>ment</u>
-er	emPLOY	emPLOY<u>er</u>

Other common suffixes *do* affect word stress. These suffixes can help you predict where stress falls in words.

Rule 8-1

These common suffixes begin with "i". Listen. What happens to the stress?

-ity	MAjor	maJOr<u>ity</u>
-ion	apPLY	appliCA<u>tion</u>
-ic	ATHlete	athLEt<u>ic</u>
-ian	LIbrary	liBRAr<u>ian</u>

 The main stress moves to the syllable *before* these suffixes beginning with "i."

Note: See Appendix 3 for a more complete list of suffixes that affect word stress.

Exercise 1 Say these words *with* the teacher or the speaker on tape. Open your fist on the stressed syllable.

va – CA – tion

-ion	**-ity**	**-ic**
		-ical
vaCAtion	possiBIlity	heROic
adDICtion	sensiTIvity	arTIStic
eduCAtion	reAlity	ecoNOmic
perFECtion	persoNAlity	roMANtic
deCIsion	seCUrity	poLItical
tuItion	elecTRIcity	CRItical

_____	_____	_____
_____	_____	_____
_____	_____	_____

Place each of the following words in the correct column above. Circle the stressed syllables.

gra du A tion	opportunity	allergic
information	organic	community
mechanic	university	permission

Check your answers with your teacher or use a dictionary. Say the words with your partner. Open your fist or give your partner a high-five on the stressed syllables.

gra - du - A - tion

Exercise 2 *Student A:* Begin each sentence. *Student B:* Close your book. Finish the sentence with a word that ends in *-ian*. Stress the syllable before *-ian*.

1. Someone who lives in Canada is a ____CaNAdian.____
2. Someone who works in a library is a _____.
3. Someone who works in politics is a _____.
4. Someone who studies history is a _____.
5. Someone who fixes electrical problems is an _____.

SWITCH ROLES

6. Someone born in Italy usually speaks _____.
7. Someone who plays music is a _____.
8. Someone who creates magic is a _____.
9. Someone who plans people's diets is a _____.
10. Someone who eats mostly vegetables is a _____.

🎧 *2, 27* Now listen to the teacher or the speaker on the audio say the sentences. Repeat.

Calvin and Hobbs © (1987) Watterson. Dist. By UNIVERSAL PRESS SYNDICATE. Reprinted with permission. All Rights Reserved.

Exercise 3 Fill in the blanks with the correct spelling. Each blank is the unstressed vowel sound schwa /ə/.

Example: <u>o</u> PIN ion

1. __mBRELla
2. c__nCLUsion
3. defiNIt__n
4. s__gGEStion
5. TEl__vision

Check your answers. Review the Helpful Hint! in Chapter 7.
Repeat the words.

[2, 28]

Choose two words from the list above. Write the word in the parentheses and use it in a sentence you might say in everyday life. Look up and say the sentences to your partner. Lengthen the stressed syllables. Reduce the unstressed syllables.

Example: (opinion) *What's your opinion of that neighborhood?*

1. ( ) _____

2. ( ) _____

[2, 29]
Rule 8-2 Listen to the words with these suffixes. Notice the main stress.

  -ese   ChinESE
  -eer   voluntEER
  -ee   trainEE

☑ **The main stress usually falls *on* these suffixes.**

Exercise 4 With your partner, circle the stressed syllable in the italicized words. Take turns saying the sentences.

Example: Some of my friends *volunteer* at the Homeless Shelter.

1. This DVD player has a two-year *guarantee*.
2. My father changed *careers* when he was *forty*.
3. Our new *trainees* are *energetic* and *enthusiastic*.
4. The *engineers* are making excellent *progress*.
5. How do you say "Excuse me" in *Japanese*?
6. The *referee* stopped a fight at the *basketball game* last night.
7. Gabriela has her *degree* in *mathematics*.
8. Several of my *classmates* are *Vietnamese*.

Check your answers.
Repeat each sentence.

2, 30

A Helpful Hint!

What is the best way to improve pronunciation? There is not just one answer. But **self-monitoring** is effective for almost everyone! What is self-monitoring?

Self-monitoring is listening to and evaluating your pronunciation. First, record your speech. Then listen to it. But listen for just one or two features you have already studied.

If you do this regularly, your everyday speech will begin to improve. You have been self-monitoring in your *Pronunciation to Go* assignments. In Exercise 5, you will do more self-monitoring.

Exercise 5 Paragraph reading.

Step 1: Read the paragraph silently. Finish the paragraph.

Step 2: Circle the stressed syllables in the underlined words. The first one is done for you.

Step 3: Practice the paragraph aloud. Then record yourself reading it.

Step 4: Listen. Monitor stress in the underlined words. If correct, mark with a check (✓). If incorrect, mark with an (✗). Add up the number that are correct.

Step 5: Re-record. Listen. Monitor and add up the number that are correct again.

CLASSROOM CONDUCT

Most com(mu)nity colleges and universities in the United States have a code for classroom conduct. They expect students to conduct themselves in a professional way. For example, students should have cell phones turned off. Students should be sure that homework is handed in on time. Students should not have conversations that disrupt instruction. On the other hand, many teachers expect active discussion about the class material. They base part of the grade on class participation. Some teachers ask students to help create a contract for classroom behavior. If I had that opportunity, I would suggest these guidelines:

1. _____

2. _____

3. _____

Recording 1: _____ correct/21 words   Recording 2: _____ correct/21 words

---

At any time, listen to the speaker on the audio read the paragraph. Practice by reading *with* the speaker on the audio.

Optional: With your class, create a contract for classroom conduct.

Extend Your Skills . . . to a short oral presentation

Who is your everyday hero? Who inspires you? Nominate someone to carry the Olympic torch. Your nominee can be a friend, co-worker, family member, or neighbor.

Step 1: Draft or outline a short 75–100 word speech that describes your nominee. Why does this person inspire you? How does this person reflect the best qualities in humanity?

▲ Guri

Model Speech:

My nominee is my neighbor Guri. She got her degree in electrical engineering from the University of Texas. She works and has a 3-year old daughter. Life is busy for Guri, but she is always enthusiastic and ready to help anybody at anytime. She finds time to volunteer 20 hours a week with a charity that designs free websites for nonprofit organizations. Her responsibility is to coordinate projects. Guri's generosity inspires me. She's a role model for working mothers.

Step 2: Circle or highlight words that follow word stress rules from Chapters 7 and 8. Can you find any more?

Step 3: Review stressed syllables in the words you highlighted:

Examples from model above:

nomiNEE	WEBsites	deGREE	PROjects
volunTEER	organiZAtions	engiNEERing	responsiBIlity
enthusiAStic	geneROsity		

Step 4: Make notes or notecards to use for your speech. Do not memorize or read your speech. Practice your speech. Remember *-s* and *-ed* endings too.

Model Notes:
Nominee — Guri   1
      EE @ UT
   Works & 3yr daugh

Hectic but enthus./ready to help

Vol 20 hrs/wk   2
  Des'gn websites
   -coord proj.

   Inspired by generos'y
   Role model—work moth

My Speech:

_____

_____

_____

_____

_____

_____

My Notes (Transfer your notes to real index cards, use an overhead projector, or give a Power Point Presentation):

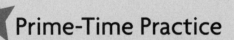

Step 5: Bring a photograph or something that interests you to show class members! Practice. Give your speech to your class.

⭐ Prime-Time Practice

Add five words to your personal word list in Appendix 1. They should be **long** words with **three or more syllables.** They can be from work, school, or everyday life. Look the words up in your dictionary. Or, go to a talking dictionary website to *hear* the words pronounced correctly.

Show number of syllables and main stress. Write a sentence you would say with the words.

Example: occupation   oc-cu-PA-tion   What is your occupation?

Say each word and sentence three times slowly and silently. Bring your words to class. Brainstorm ways to practice the pronunciation of new words.

Basic Rhythm—Stressed Words

Words have strong and weak beats:	. —— . com- PU - ter
So do sentences:	. —— . We KNEW her.

The pattern of strong and weak beats gives English its **rhythm**.

In this chapter, you will learn about basic rhythm patterns in phrases and sentences.

You will also learn . . .

- Which words are stressed
- Why these words are stressed

Get Set!

Your college sends you messages on your mobile phone. The message below is too long to fit on your screen.

Make the message shorter. Cross out unnecessary words. Keep only the words you need to convey the message. Rewrite the message.

Full Message

Shorter Text Message

Classes will be cancelled on Tuesday. We will be repairing broken pipes. There will be an update at 4 P.M.

How many words did you remove? _____ How many did you keep? _____

What kinds of words did you remove? _____

What kinds of words did you keep? _____

Compare your short text message with your partner's.

79

Listen!

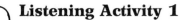

Listening Activity 1

Part A Listen to your teacher or the speaker on the audio read the poem. Pay attention to the rhythm—the pattern of strong and weak beats.

HI. How ARE you today?   by Jeff Moss

I'm FEELing very HORrible

And LOW and MEAN and MAD

And DREADful and dePLORable

And ROTten, SICK, and SAD

And NASty and unBEARable

And HATEful, VILE, and BLUE

But THANKS a lot for ASKing

And please TELL me HOW are YOU?

Part B Listen again. The strong words are easy to hear. The weak, shaded words are harder to hear. Tap your hand or snap your fingers on the strong beats.

HI. How ARE you today?

I'm FEELing very HORrible

And LOW and MEAN and MAD

And DREADful and dePLORable

And ROTten, SICK, and SAD

And NASty and unBEARable

And HATEful, VILE, and BLUE

But THANKS a lot for ASKing

And please TELL me HOW are YOU?

Listening Activity 2

Part A Listen to the conversation. Half the words are missing.

Student A: _____ was your _____ in _____?

Student B: I _____ a _____. _____ about _____?

Student A: A _____. I'm in _____. I _____ a _____ to _____ to _____.

Student B: You'll be _____. You can _____ _____ in the _____.

Can you guess what the conversation is about?   Yes ☐ No ☐

Part B Listen to the same conversation. Now the other half of the words are missing.

Student A: What ___ ___ grade ___ chemistry?

Student B: ___ think ___ B. How ___ yours?

Student A: ___ D! ___ ___ trouble. ___ need ___ C ___ apply ___ nursing.

Student B: ___ ___ fine! ___ ___ retake chemistry ___ ___ summer.

Can you guess what the conversation is about?   Yes ☐ No ☐

Part C Now listen to the whole conversation. Pay attention to the rhythm—both the stressed and unstressed parts.

Student A: What was your grade in chemistry?

Student B: I think a *B*. How about yours?

Student A: A *D*! I'm in trouble. I need a *C* to apply to nursing.

Student B: You'll be fine! You can retake chemistry in the summer.

What kinds of words have more stress and stand out?

What kinds of words are unstressed and shaded?

Compare your answers with your partner's.

Rules and Practices

The rhythm of everyday speech is *not* as regular as the rhythm of poetry. But sentences have a basic pattern of stress and unstress.

Rule 9-1
Content words are usually strong or stressed. Content words offer listeners the most information.

Example: WHO can HELP me with my CHEmistry? It's REALLy HARD.

Content Words:	*Noun*	*Main Verbs*	*Adjectives*	*Adverbs*	*Interjections*	*Question Words*	*Neg. Aux.*
	chemistry	help	hard	really	Wow!	who	can't

Rule 9-2
Function words are usually weak or unstressed. Function words make sentences grammatically correct.

Example: PEter was BORN in GERmany, and he can SPEAK THREE LANguages.

Function Words:	*Articles*	*Prepositions*	*Pronouns*	*Aux. Verbs*	*Conjunctions*
	a, the	in, to	he, she	was, can	but, and

Exercise 1 Circle the content words (or the stressed syllables of the content words).

Example: It's (closed) on (Mon)days.

1. Do you want me to call you?
2. Did you sign a lease?
3. Camilla and Claudio are engaged.
4. What do you want?
5. I'm not happy with my new car.

Compare your answers with your partner's answers. Check your answers. Listen. Repeat the sentences.

2, 37

Exercise 2 Classroom Expressions. With a partner, circle the content words (or the stressed syllables of the content words).

1. What's the answer to number two?
2. I'm sorry. I can't come on Monday.
3. Can I borrow your eraser?
4. Could I share your book?
5. Whose turn is it?
6. Would you mind checking my composition?
7. I was late because I overslept.
8. What's the past tense of "write"?
9. Could you explain the directions?
10. I missed the test because I was sick.

Check your answers.
Listen and repeat the sentences. Make the stressed words and syllables l-o-n-g and clear.

Write two of your own classroom expressions below. Circle the stressed words or syllables. Share your expressions with the class.

11. _____

12. _____

Exercise 3 Children learn the rhythm of the language through rhymes.

Part A Listen to the rhythm.

_____ . _____ .

HUMPty DUMPty

_____ . . _____

SAT on a WALL

_____ . _____ .

HUMPty DUMPty

_____ . . _____

HAD a great FALL

Say the rhyme with the teacher or speaker two times.

Part B Say the rhymes and sentences with your teacher or the speaker on tape. The common phrases have the same rhythm as the rhyme.

_____ . _____ .

HUMPty DUMPty
Nice to meet you.
What's for dinner?
What's the matter?
How's it going?
Just a minute.
Call your mother.

_____ . . _____

SAT on a WALL
What do you do?
Where are you from?
What do you want?
All you can eat.
Give me a break.
How do you do?

Something to Think About!

Music and poetry have rhythm. So does language. Every language has its own rhythm. English has strong beats and weak beats. Many other languages have more equal beats. What happens if you give equal emphasis to all words in English?

1. All words sound equally important—important words get lost.
2. You might sound angry or impatient—even if you are not!

To make content words easier to hear, make them long and clear. Make function words short and weak. The next two exercises will help you contrast strong and weak beats.

Exercise 4 Say the sentences with your teacher or the speaker on the audio. The sentences have three strong beats. Add function words, but keep the same time. Tap your pencil in time with the beats.

tap		*tap*		*tap*
▼		▼		▼
1. DENtists		FIX		TEETH.
The DENtists		FIX	her	TEETH.
The DENtists	have	FIXed	her	TEETH.
The DENtists	have been	FIXing	her	TEETH.

tap		*tap*		*tap*
▼		▼		▼
2. TEACHers		GIVE		TESTS.
The TEACHers		GIVE	the	TESTS.
The TEACHers	will	GIVE	the	TESTS.
The TEACHers	are	GIVing	the	TESTS.
The TEACHers	should have	GIVen	the	TESTS.

tap		*tap*		*tap*
▼		▼		▼
3. JOE		EATS		CHEESE.
JOE	will	EAT	the	CHEESE.
JOseph	will	EAT	the	CHEESE.
JOseph	will be	EATing	the	CHEESE.
JOseph	will be	EATing	the	CHEESEcake.

Say the sentences again. This time, begin with the last sentence in each set.

Exercise 5 With a partner, complete these expressions. Then practice saying them. Each phrase has two strong beats. Pronounce *as* like /əz/.

Examples: She's as WHITE as <u>a GHOST</u>.
He's as BUsy as <u>a BEE</u>.

1. It's as SWEET as	_____	a. a BIRD
2. She's as WISE as	_____	b. a FEAther
3. He EATS like	_____	c. an OWL
4. He's as QUIet as	_____	d. a RUG
5. She SMOKES like	_____	e. HOney
6. It's as FLAT as	_____	f. a MOUSE
7. He LIES like	_____	g. a CHIMney
8. It's as LIGHT as	_____	h. a PANcake
9. It's as SMOOTH as	_____	i. ICE
10. It's as COLD as	_____	j. SILK

Check your answers.
Say the phrases after the teacher or the speaker on the audio.

2, 43

Exercise 6 Members of your class form groups who work for the campus radio station. Each group will work on one of the announcements below.

Choose one person from your group to read the announcement. Help your reader mark the stressed words and syllables. Help your reader use good rhythm patterns.

Announcement 1: Registration for summer classes will begin on Friday, April 30th.

Announcement 2: Students may not register for classes by phone.

Announcement 3: The power will be out on August 23rd from 6 A.M. to 5 P.M.

Announcement 4: The main entrance to campus will be closed from June 19th to September 20th.

Announcement 5: Drama Club will meet on Thursday from 2:00 to 3:00 in Room 124, Kell Hall.

Cover the announcements when they are read. Take notes on the *important* pieces of information. Write primarily content words. Abbreviate when possible. You may be asked to repeat the announcement from your notes.

NOTES

Announcement 1: <u>Regis sum classes beg Fri 4/30</u>

Announcement 2: _____

Announcement 3: _____

Announcement 4: _____

Announcement 5: _____

Communicative Practice ... Post-it™ notes

Part A Read the poem.

This Is Just to Say   by William Carlos Williams

I have eaten
the plums
that were in
the icebox

and which
you were probably
saving
for breakfast

Forgive me
they were delicious
so sweet
and so cold

Who would you write a message like this to? Where would you put it?
Finish marking the stressed words and syllables in the poem. Check your answers.

Read the poem with the speaker on the audio. Or read it chorally with your teacher.

2, 44

Part B Do you write notes? Where do you put them?

Many people post notes on the refrigerator. Notes on refrigerators are easily seen.

Here are some sample reminders you might write *or* say. Mark the stresses. Practice saying the reminders.

Now write three of your own notes or reminders. Mark the stresses.

Share your messages with your small group. Make the more important words easier for your listeners to hear!

Basic Rhythm—Reduced Words

Function words are sometimes hard to hear. They are *reduced* so that the important content words stand out.

> . —— . —— . . ——
>
> You've SHUT the DOOR on my HAND!

In this chapter you will learn . . .

- What reduced words sound like.
- How reduced words are weakened.

Get Set!

Listen to one-half of a telephone conversation. Circle the words in parentheses that you hear. Check your answers. Or work with a partner as follows.

Student A: You are on the phone. You are planning a party for your friend, Sam. Turn to page 98. Read your half of the conversation.

Student B: You are listening to Student A talk on the phone. You can hear only his half of the conversation. Circle the words in parentheses that you hear.

The party'll be on Sunday in the Terrace Apartments.

That's right . . . (427, 4 to 7).

I (can, can't) take you.

I (can, can't) pick you up before noon.

We're having salad (in, and) sandwiches.

I'll ask (for, four) volunteers to help clean up.

Victor (can, can't) come, but he (can, can't) get the gift.

Don't worry. Sam'll love it. Snakes are quiet. And you only have to feed them once a month!

Compare what *Student A* said and *Student B* heard. Write the words that were misunderstood:

_____   _____

_____   _____

Listen!

Listening Activity 1 The teacher or the speaker on the audio will say sentence a. or b. Circle the one you hear.

Examples: a. I'll ASK for volunTEERS to help.
(b.) I'll ASK FOUR volunTEERS to help.

1. a. It's 4 to 7 (FOUR to SEVEN -- *time*).
   b. It's 4 2 7 (FOUR TWO SEVEN – *street number*).

2. a. We can   TALK.
   b. We CAN'T TALK.

3. a. It's for   EYES.
   b. It's FOUR EYES.

4. a. This is to   CLEAN.
   b. This is TOO CLEAN!

5. a. What's H to O?
   b. What's H_2O? (water)

Check your answers.
Now listen to both a. and b. Can you hear a difference in rhythm?

Listening Hint

Do native speakers speak too fast? Many students think so. The problem isn't just speed, however. Native speakers also reduce function words. Function words get lost in conversations. Students get frustrated.

As speech gets more casual, function words get harder to hear.

Formal	We should <u>həve</u> called him.
↓	We should <u>əv</u> called <u>əm.</u>
Casual	We should <u>ə</u> called <u>əm.</u>

It is not poor English to use reduced words. They are a part of English rhythm. When you listen to English, don't try to hear every word clearly. Pay more attention to the stressed words. You will be a more effective listener!

Rules and Practices

Function words have two forms—full forms and reduced forms.

Full forms are easy to hear, but they are not common. We use full forms when function words are

- Spoken alone.   <u>to</u>
- At the end of a phrase.   Who are you writing <u>to</u>?
- Emphasized.   Don't take it <u>from</u> her; give it <u>to</u> her.

Reduced forms are more common, but they are harder to hear.

✔ **Rule 10-1**

Reduced forms are short. Sounds are often lost. Vowels often change to /ə/ or /ɪ/.

Examples: Can you tell him to call me?   = /kn/ /yə/ tell /əm/ /tə/ call me?

I'll have the soup and sandwich. = I'll have the soup /ɪn/ sandwich.

Why did the server misunderstand the customer?

Common Function Words

Full Form	Reduced Form	Example
a	/ə/	a book
and	/ən/, /ɪn/, /n/	soup and sandwich
as	/əz/	as busy as a bee
are	/ər/	The cookies are done.
can	/kən/, /kn/	I can go.
for	/fər/	It's for you.
have	/əv/, /v/, /ə/	They should have gone.
her	/ər/	Give her the book.
him	/əm/, /ɪm/	Call him.
in	/ɪn/, /ən/	She's in her room.
of	/əv/, /ə/ *	all of us; cup of tea
or	/ər/	morning or afternoon
to	/tə/	Go to school.

Note: Use /əv/ before words that begin with vowel sounds: *all* /əv/ *us*. Use /ə/ before words that begin with consonant sounds: *cup* /ə/ *tea*.

Some reduced words sound alike. Using the box above, complete the grid.

1. /ə/ = ___a___ ___have___ ___of___	**3.** /ən/ = _____ _____
2. /əv/ = _____ _____	**4.** /ər/ = _____ _____ _____

Exercise 1 Read the sentences. Guess which function word is missing – *and, are, for, of, or,* or *to.*

[2, 48] Listen to the teacher or the speaker on the audio read the sentences. Write the word you hear.

1. I need a room _____ two nights.
2. All the rooms _____ full.
3. Could I talk _____ Farhad?
4. The phone's _____ you.
5. Let's go out _____ eat.
6. When _____ you graduating?
7. I want a bowl _____ soup.
8. I'd like a burrito _____ a salad.
9. He's going to India _____ Thailand.
10. Is he leaving on Monday _____ Tuesday?
11. Good idea! I didn't think _____ that.
12. Window _____ aisle seat?

Check your answers.
[2, 49] Listen again. Pay attention to the reduced forms and repeat.

Exercise 2 Match the container to the food. Complete the phrase with a word from the box.

| COFfee | CHIPS | KETchup | BREAD | MILK | CEreal |

Example: LOAF of _____BREAD_____

1. POUND of _____

2. BOTtle of _____

3. QUART of _____

4. BOX of _____

5. BAG of _____

Check your answers.
Repeat the phrases after the teacher or the speaker on the audio. Reduce *of* to /ə/. Link the words.

Example: GALlon ə GAS

Exercise 3 Find foods that go together. Fill in the blanks with words from the box.

| MEATballs | ICE cream | SANDwich | VINegar | EGGS |
| PEPper | toMAto | CHEESE | BUTter | CHIPS |

1. macaRONi and _____

2. SOUP and _____

3. LETtuce and _____

4. FISH and _____

5. OIL and _____

6. BREAD and _____

7. CAKE and _____

8. SALT and _____

9. spaGHETti and _____

10. BAcon and _____

Check your answers.
Repeat the phrases after the teacher or the speaker on the audio. Reduce *and* to /ən/. Link the words.

Example: CHEESE ən CRACKers

What are *your* favorite food combinations? Write them below. Mark the stressed syllables. In a small group, talk about your favorite food combinations. Reduce the word *and*.

_____

_____

_____

Pronunciation to Go . . . *Business Slang and Idioms*

Slang and idioms appear on the TOEFL. Many expressions have reduced forms.

Listen to the expressions. Ask native speakers how they would use these expressions. Share the responses with your class.

1. an arm and a leg
   /ən/   /ən/ /ə/

Updating the computer system will cost *an arm and a leg*.

Notes: _____

2. bone to pick
   /tə/

I have a *bone to pick* with that client. She still hasn't paid her bill.

Notes: _____

3. piece of cake
   /ə/

That project was a *piece of cake*.

Notes: _____

4. up to speed
   /tə/

After a long vacation, it's hard to get back *up to speed*.

Notes: _____

5. good to go
   /tə/

Our bags are packed and we have our plane tickets—we're *good to go*!

Notes: _____

Rule 10-2

Listen to these examples. Notice what happens to the function words *her* and *he*.

Example: Send her an application.   *sounds like*   Sender an application.

Example: Will he tell the truth?   *sounds like*   Willy tell the truth.

☑ **When the function words *her*, *he*, *him*, *his*, *have*, *has*, or *had* occur in the middle of a phrase, the "h" often disappears.**

Exercise 4 Close your book and listen to the teacher or the speakers on the audio read the following conversation. Listen again and write the word you hear—*her*, *he*, *he's*, *him*, *his*, *have*, or *has*.

The Realtor

A: Where does __*he*__ work?

B: He works with _____ father. They _____ worked together for ten years.

A: What's _____ do?

B: He sells real estate. He _____ sold more than 200 homes.

A: Sounds like _____ successful!

B: He sells a lot of houses to family and friends. In fact, he _____ sold homes to _____ sister, _____ cousin, and _____ aunt.

A: Are they happy with their homes?

B: His sister loves _____ house and so does _____ aunt. His cousin thinks _____ house is too big. He's going to help _____ find something smaller.

A: We're looking too. Maybe I should get in touch.

B: Here's _____ card. Give _____ a call.

Check your answers.

Listen again and say the dialogue *with* the speaker on the audio. Then practice the dialog with a partner.

Rule 10-3 *Can* and *can't* are easily confused. What is the difference?

.   .   ———   .

You can trust him.   (can = /kən/ or /kn/)

.   ———   ———   .

You can't trust him. (can't = /kænt/)

☑ ***Can* is unstressed; the vowel sounds like /ə/ or is omitted.
Can't is stressed; the vowel is a clear /æ/.**

Exercise 5 Listen to the teacher or the speaker on the audio say the sentence with *can* or *can't*. Circle 👍 for *can* and 👎 for *can't*.

	can	can't
Examples: I (can, can't) take you.	(👍)	👎
I (can, can't) pick you up before noon.	👍	(👎)
1. You (can, can't) have pets in your apartment.	👍	👎
2. You (can, can't) extend your visa.	👍	👎
3. I (can, can't) come to your party.	👍	👎
4. I (can, can't) help you now.	👍	👎
5. You (can, can't) smoke here.	👍	👎
6. I (can, can't) hear you.	👍	👎
7. You (can, can't) return items at this store.	👍	👎
8. I (can, can't) see that you have lost weight.	👍	👎

Check your answers.
Repeat after the speaker.

Optional: Student A: Say each sentence above with *can* or *can't*. *Student B:* Give an appropriate answer. Switch roles.

Example: A: You can have pets in your apartment.
              B: That's good news! I can keep my rabbit.

Exercise 6 Find people in your class who *can* and *can't* do the following.

Example: A: /kn/ *you cook?*

_____ Gu _____ ((can), can't) cook.

1. _____ (can, can't) speak three languages.

2. _____ (can, can't) write poetry.

3. _____ (can, can't) play an instrument.

4. _____ (can, can't) play soccer.

5. _____ (can, can't) give CPR.

6. _____ (can, can't) fix cars.

7. _____ (can, can't) ski.

8. _____ (can, can't) sing.

9. _____ (can, can't) sail a boat.

10. _____ (can, can't) fly a plane.

Now one student reports on the first item. The next student reports on the second item and so on. Class members nod if they hear *can* and shake their heads if they hear *can't*.

Example: Gu can cook.   *or*   Gu can't cook.

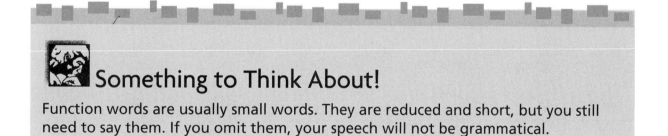

Something to Think About!

Function words are usually small words. They are reduced and short, but you still need to say them. If you omit them, your speech will not be grammatical.

Communicative Activity . . . finish the conversation

With a partner, create the other half of the phone conversation found at the beginning of the chapter. Mark the stressed content words. Practice the conversation using good English rhythm.

B: _____

A: The party'll be on Sunday in the Terrace Apartments.

B: _____

A: That's right . . . 427.

B: _____

A: Sure. I can take you.

B: _____

A: No, I can't pick you up before noon.

B: _____

A: We're having salad and sandwiches.

B: _____

A: I'll probably ask for volunteers to help clean up.

B: _____

A: Victor can't come, but he can get the gift.

B: _____

A: Don't worry. Sam'll love it—snakes are quiet. And they eat only once a month!

Do a round-robin reading. Each pair in the class says one question/answer segment of the dialogue.

★ Prime-Time Practice

What is your favorite song? _____

Go online to a song lyric Web site and find the lyrics.

Write your favorite line and bring it to class. _____

_____

Share your favorite line with the class. Use English rhythm patterns.

Focus Words

You have learned about basic rhythm—weak beats and strong beats. But one key word in every phrase is stronger than the others. It is the **focus.**

Part of a Job Interview . . .

A: So you've comPLEted TWO YEARS of **COL**lege.

B: Actually, **THREE** YEARS.

A: And your MAjor was engi**NEE**ring.

B: Yes, **CI**vil engiNEEring.

In this chapter, you will learn about focus words.

You will learn . . .

- Why speakers emphasize focus words
- How speakers emphasize focus words

Get Set!

With a partner, compare the colleges below. Underline the differences.

Linwood Community College

<u>two</u>-year college

public college

in large city

29,000 students
    10% out-of-state
    20% international

Tuition: $1,000 per semester

Admission Rate: 90%

Walton College

<u>four</u>-year college

private college

in small city

1,000 students
    52% out-of-state
    6% international

Tuition: $6,000 per semester

Admission Rate: 70%

Discuss which college you would prefer. Why?

One use of focus is to make contrasts. Listen to the examples below.

Listen!

Listening Activity 1 Listen to the teacher or the speaker on the audio. Focus words are marked with a large dot •.

        •   •

1. Linwood's a PUBlic college, but Walton's PRIvate.

        •   •

2. Linwood's a TWO-year college, and Walton's a FOUR-year college.

Did you hear the emphasis on the focus words? If not, listen again.

Listening Activity 2   Listen. Which word in each phrase gets the most emphasis? Put a dot • above the focus word in each phrase.

1. Linwood's located in a large city, but Walton's in a small city.

2. Linwood's tuition is one thousand a semester, but Walton's is six thousand.

Check your answers.
Listen again.

Listening Activity 3
Part A Listen to the teacher or the speaker on the audio hum these sentences. What makes you notice the focus words?

1. Linwood has a HUGE student body, but Walton has a SMALL one.

2. Linwood's admission rate is NINEty percent, but Walton's is SEventy percent.

The focus words jump up in pitch. They also are longer.
Listen again.

Focus words in general have a major pitch change. Sometimes the pitch jumps down but usually the pitch jumps up.

Part B Listen to the teacher or the speaker hum these sentences. Then hum *with* the teacher or speaker on the audio.

1. Linwood has a ^HUGE student body, but Walton has a ^SMALL one.

2. Linwood's admission rate is ^NINEty percent, but Walton's is ^SEventy percent.

Rules and Practices

Focus words are the *most important* words in a conversation.

Normally, the focus is the *last content word* of each sentence or phrase. This is often true at the beginning of a conversation

> *Normal Focus*: Walton's a four-year CÖLlege / located in a small CÏty./
>
> It has about a thousand STÜdents / and costs six thousand a seMËSter./

But focus can move to other words for special reasons. Maybe the speaker wants to reply to a previous statement. Or maybe the speaker wants to make a contrast between **four** and **two** and **small** and **big.**

> *Special focus:* Walton's a FÖUR-year college,/ not a TWÖ-year
>
> college./ And it's in a SMÄLL city / not a BÏG city./

First you will learn about *normal* or neutral focus.

The Basic Pattern: Normal Focus

Rule 11-1

The focus is usually the last content word in a phrase or sentence. Most of the time this is new information.

Example: My MAjor was engiNËEring.

Exercise 1 With a partner, put a dot above the **last** content word (or the stressed syllable of the last content word)

Examples: WHEN'S the FInal exAM?

That QUIZ was HARD.

1. I'm LEARNing to PLAY GOLF.

2. CARlos MISSED the TRAIN.

3. WHAT should we ORder for desSERT?

4. I'd LIKE a LATte to GO.

5. WHERE should I PARK?

Check your answers.
Now repeat each sentence after your teacher or the speaker on the audio. Did you notice? The pitch jumps up on the focus and then *glides* down.

Exercise 2 With a partner, put a dot above the **last** content word (or the stressed syllable of the last content word).

Examples: WHEN did you CALL me?

I BROUGHT my NOTES for you.

1. The TEAcher is WAITing for you.

2. The SERver was RUDE to us.

3. WHOSE NEWSpaper is this?

4. I've MISSED you.

5. WHAT'S my PASSword?

Check your answers.
Now repeat each sentence after the teacher or the speaker on the audio. Did you notice? The pitch jumps up on the focus and then *steps* down.

Exercise 3 How do you manage stress in your life? Choose five of your favorite ways. Rank them from 1 to 5.

Tell your partner what they are. Make the focus in each phrase stand out.

	Example	My Stress Busters	My Partner's Stress-Busters
• LISten to MUsic	——	——	——
• READ a BOOK	——	——	——
• WATCH TELevision	——	——	——
• GO to the MOvies	_2_	——	——
• TAKE a NAP	——	——	——
• TALK to my FAMily	——	——	——
• work OUT at the GYM	——	——	——
• TAKE a WALK	_3_	——	——
• PRACtice YOga	_4_	——	——
• SURF the WEB	——	——	——
• GO SHOPping	_5_	——	——
• TAKE a HOT BATH	_1_	——	——
• go OUT with my FRIENDS	——	——	——
Other: _____	——	——	——

Are any of your favorite stress-busters the same as your partner's? Report them to the class.

Special Focus: Changes in Focus

Focus can change from the last content word. It can move to other important words.

Rule 11-2
☑ **Use focus to introduce new information.**

Example: A: I see your major was engiNEEring.

        B: Yes, CÍvil engiNEEring.

Keep old information at a low pitch so new information will stand out.

Example: A: I CAN'T FIND the SCHEdule.

        B: WHÍCH SCHEdule?

        A: The TRÁIN SCHEdule.

Rule 11-3
☑ **Use focus to emphasize answers to Wh-questions.**

Examples: A: WHICH CAR is YOURS?

        B: The BLUE one.

        A: WHO TOLD you about my NEW JOB?

        B: RÁJ TOLD me about it.

Exercise 4 Practice these dialogues with a partner. Make the focus words jump out. Listen to the models at any time.

Dialogue 1

A: Wake UP! I HEAR a NOISE!

B: What KIND of NOISE?

A: A SCRAtching NOISE. I'm REALly aFRAID!

B: It's PRObably the CAT. Go BACK to SLEEP.

Dialogue 2

A: WHAT are you WATCHing?

B: A reAlity show.*

A: It SEEMS like they're ALL REALITY SHOWS.

B: Well, THIS one's REALly DIFferent.

A: THAT'S because you're WATching a comMERcial!

Dialogue 3 Mark the focus in each phrase. Check your answers with your teacher. Then practice the dialogue with your partner.

A: Let's go to Italy.

B: I love Italy. But we don't have the money.

A: Maybe we could borrow the money.

---

*ReAlity show is a compound noun like STOCK market, CELL phone, etc.

Dialogue 4 Mark the focus in each phrase. Check your answers with your teacher. Then practice the dialogue with your partner.

B: Let's order a pizza.

A: But I'm on a diet.

B: Maybe you can break your diet.

Dialogue 5 Mark the focus in each phrase. Check your answers with your teacher. Then practice the dialogue with your partner.

A: I'll see you on Thursday.

B: No, I'm off on Thursday.

A: That's right. See you on Friday.

A Helpful Hint!

Do you move to the rhythm of music? Do you clap your hands? Or tap your feet? Or move your head? Most speakers move to the rhythm of the language. English speakers almost always move part of the upper body when they use focus.

When you practice focus, add movement. As you say the focus word or syllable,

- use a natural gesture, or
- stretch a rubber band vertically, or
- nod your head slightly, or
- raise your eyebrow.

Exercise 5 Go back to Exercise 2. Try at least two of the strategies above.

Which strategy was most effective for you? _____

Rule 11-4

☑ **Use focus to disagree or make corrections.**

Examples: A: Weimin's house is the second one on the RIGHT.

B: I thought it was the THIRD one.

A: What a cute little BOY!

B: She's a GIRL!

Exercise 6 *Student A*: Say statement A. *Student B*: Look at the **Get Set!** box at the beginning of the chapter. Correct Student A's statements.

Example: Student A: Linwood's **SMALL**.

          Student B: No, it's _____LARGE_____.

Optional: Student A can monitor Student B's use of focus in the response.

1. A: I think you can go to Linwood for four **YEARS**.

    B: No, only _____TWO_____ years.

2. A: Somebody told me Linwood has about 39,000 **STU**dents.

    B: Actually, it has _29_,000 students.

3. A: I heard fifty percent of Linwood's students are inter**NA**tional.

    B: No, it's _____TWENty_____ percent.

4. A: My friend said the admission rate at Linwood was around sixty per**CENT**.

    B: It's _____NINEty_____ percent.

5. A: I'm pretty sure Linwood is in a small **CI**ty.

    B: No, it's in a _____BIG_____ city.

Exercise 7 Complete the statements with a focus word. Practice the sentences with your partner.

1. I don't WÖRK at the library. I _____ there.

2. He doesn't want toMÄto soup. He wants _____ soup.

3. My father drives a brand NËW car, but my grandfather drives an _____ one.

4. Miguel LÏKES cold weather, but his girlfriend _____ it.

5. My children ÄLways watch TV, but I _____ watch it.

Report your answers to the class.

Think of similar contrasts in your life or in the lives of people you know.
Write them below.

6. _____ .

7. _____ .

8. _____ .

Mark the focus words. Report your answers to your class.

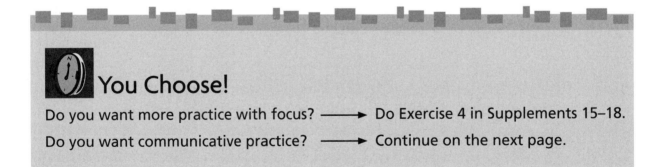

You Choose!

Do you want more practice with focus? ⟶ Do Exercise 4 in Supplements 15–18.

Do you want communicative practice? ⟶ Continue on the next page.

Communicative Practice . . . comparing class notes

You and your partner are studying for a history quiz. Some of your notes are below.

Step 1: Compare your notes. Underline the differences.

Step 2: Decide who is correct. Then make corrections in your notes.

Example: Let's see . . . I have **ROB**ert Kennedy /and you have **JOHN** Kennedy . . ./

Major Events of the 20th Century
Student A: Notes

Titanic sank 1902

Wright Bros.1st flight 1903—lasted 12 sec.

Great Depression—1930s

WW 2 ended 1945

Pres. Rob't Kennedy
        assassinated—1963

1st person walked on moon—1969

Berlin Wall fell 1989

Major Events of the 20th Century
Student B: Notes

Titanic sank 1902

Wright Bros 1st flight '03—3 sec.

Gr Depression occurred 1930s

WW 2 end 1945

Pres. John Kennedy assass'd
        in '63

1st person walked in space 1969

Berlin Wall fell 1989

Step 3: Report your corrections to the class.

A Helpful Hint!

Athletes use silent mental practice before they compete. Gymnasts mentally rehearse routines. Skiers imagine each part of their ski runs.

You can use silent mental practice too. Think about what you will say. Practice it silently over and over before you say it. You will speak more clearly and feel more confident.

Use silent mental practice in the next activity.

⊚ Pronunciation to Go! . . . focus to disagree or correct

Think of something you need to say to a teacher, a friend, a co-worker, or anyone else. The interaction should involve a disagreement or correction.

Step 1: Write what you will say. Mark the focus in each phrase or sentence. Examples are below.

Who will you speak to? _____

What will you say? _____

_____

_____

Example 1: (to a teacher): Could you check my quiz? You marked five wrong, and I can find only four wrong.

Example 2: (in a department store): I'd like to exchange these shoes. I need size nine, not size ten.

Example 3: (in a grocery store): I'd like paper, not plastic.

Example 4: (to a supervisor): I worked twenty-nine hours last week, but I think I was paid for twenty-five.

Step 2: Copy your sentences onto a piece of paper. Give the sentences to your teacher for feedback. When your teacher returns your paper, go to Step 3.

Step 3: Imagine yourself saying what you wrote. Say it silently over and over. Say it until you are comfortable with how it sounds and feels.

Step 4: Then say what you have practiced to your teacher, friend, or classmate. Did the silent practice help you? Report back to your class.

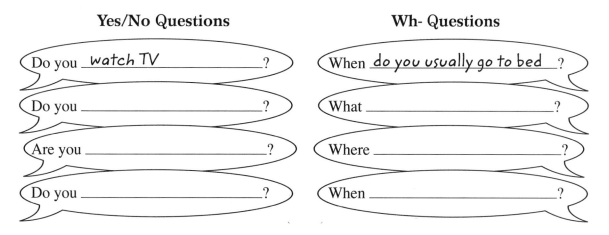

Intonation: Rising and Falling

Intonation is the tune or pitch of the voice. You learned that the pitch usually jumps up on the key word in each phrase. Then what happens?

Then the pitch continues to **rise** ↗ or it **falls** ↘.

> Did you LOCK the **DOOR**? ↗

> WHERE's the **KEY**? ↘

Each sentence or phrase ends with either a rising or falling intonation.

In this chapter, you will learn about . . .

- Basic rising intonation
- Basic falling intonation

Get Set!

You and your partner are looking for a new housemate. You will interview some people this week. What questions do you want to ask?

Yes/No Questions	Wh- Questions
Do you _watch TV_ ?	When _do you usually go to bed_ ?
Do you ____ ?	What ____ ?
Are you ____ ?	Where ____ ?
Do you ____ ?	When ____ ?

With your partner, practice asking the questions you wrote.
Did your voice rise or fall at the end of these questions?

113

Listen!

Listening Activity 1 Listen to the teacher or the speakers on the audio say the one-word dialogue. What is it about?

Listen again and circle ↘ for falling and ↗ for rising intonation.

			Fall	*Rise*
Example:	A:	Cold?	↘	(↗)
	B:	No	(↘)	↗

****

		Fall	*Rise*
A:	Tired?	↘	↗
B:	Yes.	↘	↗
A:	Why?	↘	↗
A:	Roommate.	↘	↗
B:	Roommate?	↘	↗
A:	Yes.	↘	↗
B:	Student?	↘	↗
A:	Musician.	↘	↗
B:	Pianist?	↘	↗
A:	Drummer.	↘	↗

Check your answers.

Listen again.

Listening Activity 2 Listen to the teacher or the speaker on audio ask the questions. Draw ↘ if the voice falls at the end. Draw ↗ if the voice rises at the end.

Examples: Are you a student? ↗

What year are you? ↘

1. What's your name? ☐
2. Where did you grow up? ☐
3. When do you study? ☐
4. What time do you go to bed? ☐
5. What's your major? ☐

6. Do you work? ☐
7. You live in the dorm? ☐
8. Do you like pets? ☐
9. Do you watch TV? ☐
10. Do you enjoy parties? ☐

Check your answers.
Listen again.

Rules and Practices

Rule 12-1

☑ **The intonation usually falls at the end of a statement.**

Example: We're looking for a **ROOM**mate. ↘

Did you notice? The voice jumps up on the focus and then begins to fall.

Rule 12-2

☑ **The intonation usually falls at the end of *wh*-questions that ask for new information.**

Example: What **YEAR** are you? ↘

The voice jumps up on the focus and then begins to fall.

Exercise 1 In pairs, mark the focus of each question with a •. Then take turns asking and answering the questions. *Student A* asks Question 1, *Student B* asks Question 2, and so on.

Example: A: Where are you li̇ving? ↘

 B: In the dorm.

1. What year are you?

2. What's your major?

3. Where did you grow up?

4. How much time do you spend studying?

5. When do you usually go to bed?

6. What do you like to do in your free time?

Add three *wh-* questions. Mark the focus. Ask your partner the questions.

7. _____

8. _____

9. _____

Listen to the teacher or the speaker on the audio ask Questions 1 through 6. Repeat.

3, 21

CALVIN AND HOBBES © 1992 Watterson. Dist. By UNIVERSAL PRESS SYNDICATE. Reprinted with permission. All rights reserved.

3, 22 **Rule 12-3**

✓ **In North American English, yes-no questions usually end in rising intonation.**

Example: A: Are you a **STU**dent? ↗

 B: YES. At **STATE.**

Did you notice? The voice rises on the focus word and ***then*** rises a little more.

Note: In yes-no questions, you will sometimes hear the pitch fall on the focus word before it rises.

Example: A: Do you PLAY in a **ROCK** band? ↘↗

 B: Um-hmm. I'm the **DRUM**mer.

Exercise 2 In pairs, mark the focus of the question. Take turns asking and answering the questions. *Student A* asks Question 1, *Student B* asks Question 2, and so on.

Example: A: Do you have a cãr? ↗

      B: No, I take the subway.

1. Do you watch TV?

2. Do you work?

3. Do you like pets?

4. Are you living in a dorm?

5. Do you enjoy parties?

6. Do you study a lot?

Add three yes-no questions. Mark the focus. Ask your partner the questions.

7. _____

8. _____

9. _____

Listen to the teacher or the speaker on the audio ask Questions 1 through 6. Repeat.

A Helpful Hint!

English speakers often return questions when they are getting acquainted. Here is a returned *wh*-question:

    A: Where are you **FROM**? ↘

    B: North **AF**rica. Where are **YOU** from? ↘

Returned questions are also common in everyday speech. Here is a returned yes-no question.

    A: Did you study for the **QUIZ**? ↗

    B: A **LIT**tle. Did **YOU** study? ↗

(3, 24) **Rule 12-4**

☑ **In returned questions, the focus word changes.**

Example: A: WHAT do you **DO**?

　　　　　 B: I'm a **STU**dent. WHAT do **YOU** DO?

　　　　　 A: I'm a **TOUR** guide.

Exercise 3 *Student A*: Ask the question. *Student B*: Answer the question. Return the same question. *Student A*: Answer the returned question.

Example: A: WHAT'S your **NAME**? ↘

　　　　　 B: **PE**ter. WHAT'S **YOUR** NAME? ↘

　　　　　 A: **LU**. But my **NICK**name is **JES**sie.

1. Where are you from?

2. Are you a student?

3. When did you move here?

4. Do you like living in _____?
　　　　　　　　　　　　　　 (this city or town)

SWITCH ROLES

5. What do you do?

6. Do you have a business card?

7. Do you have any children?

8. What do you do in your free time?

9. How was your weekend?

Write two more small-talk questions. Then ask your partner. Your partner should answer and return the same question to you.

10. _____

11. _____

(3, 25) Rule 12-5

☑ In choice questions, each choice receives focus. The voice rises on choice one and falls on choice two.

Example: A: What's for **DIN**ner?

B: I haven't decided. Do you want **TO**fu ↗/ or **BUR**gers? ↘

A: **BUR**gers. **DE**finitely.

Exercise 4 Take turns asking and answering the choice questions. You may listen to and repeat the models at any time.

(3, 26)

Example: big **CI**ties / small **TOWNS**

A: Do you like big **CI**ties ↗/ or small **TOWNS**? ↘

B: I guess small **TOWNS**. People are **FRIEND**lier.

1. **ROCK** music / **CLAS**sical music

2. **DRI**ving / **FLY**ing

3. **MOUN**tains / **O**cean

4. **FALL** / **SPRING**

5. paying **CASH** / using a **CRE**dit card

6. reading **NO**vels / reading **MA**gazines

7. being **MAR**ried / being **SIN**gle

8. being a **STU**dent / **WOR**king

9. **WATCH**ing sports / **PLAY**ing sports

10. Other: _____ / _____

Exercise 5 TOEFL® iBT Speaking Practice (Optional)

Question: Some people prefer going to college in a small town. Other people prefer a big city. Which of these do you prefer and why? Include details and examples to support your choice. Take 15 seconds to prepare. Take 45 seconds to respond.

Suggestion: Take 15 seconds to make notes. Write the advantages and disadvantages of the small town and the big city.

Going to college in a small town	Going to college in a big city
No public transportation	Public transportation-don't need car
More peaceful, quiet	Noisy and crowded
Boring	Alive
Less to do	More to do
Safer	More crime?

Make what you are comparing the focus (small **TOWN** and big **CI**ty). Also make the differences between the two the focus. Here are some sample sentences.

Example: I'd prefer to go to school in a small **TOWN** for several reasons. First, it might get **BOR**ing, but maybe it would be **EAS**ier to **STU**dy. If I went to school in a big **CI**ty, there would be more to **DO**, but it might be **HAR**der to study.

Use any of the topics in **Exercise 4** for more practice.

Communicative Practice . . . arranging a room

You and your partner will arrange an ideal room. With your partner, draw the furniture in the room.

You do not have to use everything. Some items (beds, chests, desks) were already in the room. You have brought other items (microwaves, mini-fridge, beanbag chair, bookcase, file cabinet, computers).

Step 1: Practice intonation in the sample statements and questions.

What did you **BRING**? ↘

What did **YOU** bring? ↘

Does this desk fit in the **COR**ner? ↗

Where should we put this **CHEST**? ↘

Should we put the television **HERE** ↗/ or **THERE** ↘?

Where do **YOU** want to put it? ↘

Step 2: *Student A*: Your items are on the left side of the page. *Student B*: Your items are the right side. Arrange your ideal room. Cross out items you do not use. Describe your room to your classmates.

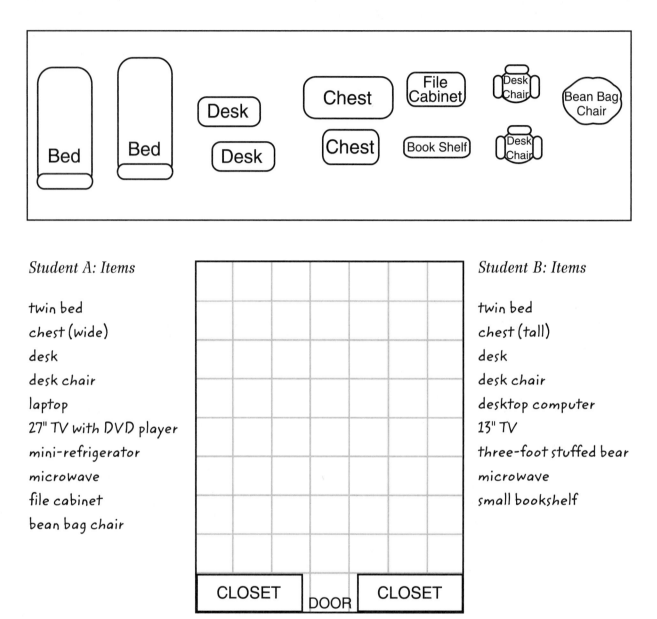

Student A: Items

twin bed
chest (wide)
desk
desk chair
laptop
27" TV with DVD player
mini-refrigerator
microwave
file cabinet
bean bag chair

Student B: Items

twin bed
chest (tall)
desk
desk chair
desktop computer
13" TV
three-foot stuffed bear
microwave
small bookshelf

Thought Groups and Pausing

A fluent *reader* reads in thought groups or phrases.

⌒   ⌒
When I went to kindergarten and had to speak English for the first time,
⌒
I became silent.

From *The Woman Warrior* by Maxine Hong Kingston

A fluent *speaker* speaks in thought groups. Each thought group has a focus.

If you'd like to make a **CALL**, / please hang **UP**/ and dial a**GAIN**./

In this chapter, you will learn . . .

- How to create thought groups
- How thought groups help listeners understand

Get Set!

The phone message below needs breaks. How would you divide the message? Put a slash (/) at the end of each thought group.

This is Miguel Rodriguez from Global Technologies I'm very sorry but I have a conflict and I can't make the meeting on Thursday Could we change it to another time Please call me at 7025427590 Thanks

Compare your thought groups with your partner's. Is there more than one right way to divide the message into thought groups?

Listen!

⌢ **Listening Activity 1** Listen to the teacher or the speaker on the audio. Mark the end
3, 27 of each thought group with a slash (/).

> This is Miguel Rodriguez from Global Technologies I'm
> very sorry but I have a conflict and I can't make the
> meeting on Thursday Could we change it to another
> time Please call me at 7025427590 Thanks

Check your answers.

⌢ Listen again. How did these thought groups compare with your thought groups in
3, 28 **Get Set!**

⌢ **Listening Activity 2** Listen to the teacher or the speaker on the audio. Mark the end
3, 29 of each thought group with a slash (/).

Example: Student ID: 276/53/2297

1. 533 Conley Road Suite 200

2. Rockwall Texas 75087

3. April 23 1982

4. 5106364441

5. R o d r i g u e z

6. www.favoritepoem.org

7. The Republicans say the Democrats will win.

8. The Republicans say the Democrats will win.

Check your answers.

⌢ Listen again.
3, 30

Rules and Practices

Rule 13-1

☑ **A thought group is a group of words that naturally go together.**

Example: I'll call you / when I finish my homework.

A thought group can also be numbers or letters that go together.

Examples: 404-/ 371-/ 8648 (*area code / prefix / number*)

Shang / hai (*city in China, spelled in syllable groups*)

5498 / Cypress Way / Apartment B (*street number, street name, apartment*)

Did you notice? We often pause briefly at the end of a thought group. That gives the listener time to take in each part of the message.

Exercise 1 *Student A*: Address this envelope to your partner's home. *Student B*: Say your name, address, city, state, and zip code. Use thought groups and pausing.

Example: Mr. Omer Ari
1025 Slaton Highway, Apt. B3
Lubbock, TX 79452

If you need to spell, divide the word into syllable groups. Take care of misunderstandings by speaking, not writing.

(3, 32) Rule 13-2

✓ **We divide longer sentences into thought groups. A thought group is a part of a sentence that makes sense.**

Example: This is Miguel Rodriguez / from Global Technologies.
         (clause)   *(prepositional phrase)*

Exercise 2 Which thought groups make more sense in each pair? Check a. or b.

Example: ☐ a. I don't exercise because I don't / have the time.
           ☑ b. I don't exercise / because I don't have the time.

1. ☐ a. It was a warm day / with gentle breezes.
     ☐ b. It was a warm day with / gentle breezes.

2. ☐ a. Could we change the meeting / to another time?
     ☐ b. Could we change the meeting to / another time?

3. ☐ a. I lost / my winter coat and bought a new one.
     ☐ b. I lost my winter coat / and bought a new one.

4. ☐ a. I didn't recognize / Jorge after he shaved off his mustache.
     ☐ b. I didn't recognize Jorge / after he shaved off his mustache.

Check your answers. Take turns reading the sentences you checked.

(3, 33) Or, listen to the teacher or the speaker on the audio say the checked sentences and repeat.

(3, 34) Rule 13-3

✓ **A thought group usually has one focus.**

Exercise 3 Match a thought group in Column 1 to a thought group in Column 2. Practice saying the sentences.

Column 1	Column 2
1. Sorry to **BO**ther you,	maybe we should get **FLU** shots.
2. As far as I **KNOW**,	who got hit by a **CAR**.
3. We heard about the **MAN**	but where did you put my **NOTE**book?
4. If I had **KNOWN**,	it's not supposed to **RAIN**.
5. To be **SAFE**,	I would have **TOLD** you.

Check your answers.
Then listen to the teacher or the speaker on the audio say each sentence. Repeat.

[3, 35]

Something to Think About!

Writers use commas and periods to mark thought groups.

Example: The grades, which were excellent, are posted online.

How do speakers mark thought groups? Speakers often pause, but they also have to use their voices.

[3, 36] **Rule 13-4**

☑ **After the focus, there is a *slight* fall in pitch—often followed by a slight rise.**

The rise tells the listener, " I am going to continue."

Example: I'm **SOR**ry / but I have a **CON**flict / and I can't make the **MEE**ting.↘

Note: At the end of thought groups, you may hear the voices of some speakers simply rise in pitch.

Example: I'm **SOR**ry ↗/ but I have a **CON**flict ↗/ and I can't make the **MEE**ting. ↘

Exercise 4 Complete each thought group with another thought group. As partners, take turns saying the sentences to each other.

Example: If Lucy is still up**SET** with you,   *take her some flowers.*

1. If you go to the **DRUG**store,   _____.

2. When you move into your new a**PART**ment,   _____.

3. Ever since his di**VORCE**,   _____.

4. If you don't like the service in a **RES**taurant,   _____.

5. The best gift I ever re**CEIVED**   _____.

Exercise 5 Use a slash mark / to divide these quotes into thought groups. Put a dot • above the focus in each thought group.

Example: HÉRE / men from the planet EÁRTH / first set foot on the MÓON, / JuLÝ /

1969 A.D. / We came in PEÁCE / for all MÁNkind.

—Plaque on moon marking the U.S. landing there, July 1969

1. The human brain starts working the moment you are born and never stops until you stand up to speak in public.

—George Jessel

2. Babies don't need a vacation but I still see them at the beach. I'll go over to them and say, "What are you doing here! You've never worked a day in your life!"

—Steven Wright

3. Your favorite quote: _____

_____

Share your answers with the class. Remember there is more than one right way to phrase the quotes.

Say the quotes chorally with your class or *with* the speakers on audio. Pause briefly after each thought group. Repeat until you can say the quotes in one voice.

★ Prime-Time Practice

1. Find the phone message that you wrote in **Pronunciation to Go!** in Chapter 4 on page 30. Copy it below.

   Message: _____

   _____

   _____

   _____

   _____

2. Use slash marks / to divide the message into thought groups.

3. Use a dot • to mark the focus of each thought group.

4. Record the message. Pause briefly at each /. Make your focus words stand out.

5. Listen to the recording. Does each thought group sound like one long word with one strong syllable? ___ YES ___ NO   If not, try again.

Extend Your Skills . . . to giving instructions

Thought groups are important when you explain how to do something, especially if you are speaking to a group.

1. Choose a simple process to teach to your class. Your process should have four or five basic steps. *(e.g., how to use a piece of equipment at work; how to cook a favorite family dish; how to measure your heart rate; how to do a favorite dance, and so forth.)*

2. Put the steps of the process on the ladder below.

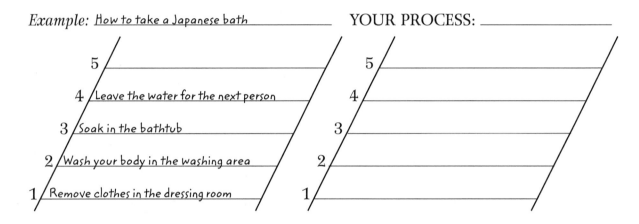

Example: How to take a Japanese bath   YOUR PROCESS: _____

5
4 / Leave the water for the next person
3 / Soak in the bathtub
2 / Wash your body in the washing area
1 / Remove clothes in the dressing room

5
4
3
2
1

3. Write one short part of the presentation.

Example: Introduction

> If you visit Japan and stay in a Japanese home, you'll need to know how to take a bath. It's very different from taking a bath in North America.

4. To create thought groups, imagine what you wrote is a poem. Arrange it into short lines. Put a dot above the focus word in each line or thought group.

If you visit Japan

and stay in a Japanese home

you'll need to know

how to take a bath.

It's very different from taking a bath

in North America.

Write a short part of your presentation here.

Arrange what you wrote as a poem here.

5. Practice reading the thought groups. Pause briefly at the end of each line.

6. Add movement to your practice. Choose a strategy from page 108 in Chapter 11. Or walk the thought groups, stepping only on each focus.

7. Practice your presentation with your partner. Introduce each step with words like *first, second, third, then, after that, the next step, the last step,* and so on. Pause after each of these words or phrases. Your partner should use the peer evaluation form in Appendix 4.

8. Give your presentation to your class. Use diagrams or photographs to make your presentation more interesting.

Example: **Step 2:** Wash be**FORE** you get in the tub.

Artwork by Haruya

Connected Speech

In written English, we separate words.

> Written English: How are you doing?

In spoken English, we connect words.

> Spoken English: Howyadoin?

The end of one word connects or links with the beginning of the next word. Words in a thought group might sound like one long word.

> **You have been practicing linking throughout** *Well Said Intro.* **In this chapter, you will learn more about . . .**
>
> - How to link words
> - How sounds get changed, lost, or added when we link

Get Set!

The dialogue below is hard to read. It is written the way it would *sound* in everyday speech.

What are the speakers saying? Write down your guesses. You can listen to the teacher or the speakers on the audio say the dialogue if you wish.

The Driver's License

Fred has just returned from taking a driving test. This is the third time he has tried to pass the test and get a license.

Spoken English	**Written English**
What we hear:	What we see:
A: Dija gedit?	*Did you get it?*
B: Godit!	
A: Whada relief! Bedit major day.	
B: Sherdid. Wanna ride home?	
A: Thanks anyway—I think I'll walk.	

Discuss your guesses with other members of the class. Then check the answers below. What sound changes surprise you the most?

Listen!

Listening Activity 1   Listen to the teacher or the speaker on the audio build the sentences. Do the last two sentences in each group sound the same?

1. cup
   cup a love
   like a cup a love
   like a **cup a love** egg rolls
   I'd like a **cup a love** egg rolls.
   I'd like a **couple of** egg rolls.

2. major
   major bed
   major bed this morning
   Who **major** bed this morning?
   Who **made your** bed this morning?

3. Andy won
   Andy won the chess game
   Andy won the chess game too.
   And he won the chess game too.

4. often
   often running
   The horses are **often** running.
   The horses are **off and** running.

5. the mall
   of the mall
   the fairest of the mall
   Who's the fairest of **the mall?**
   Who's the fairest of **them all**?

Rules and Practices

Words in thought groups are linked. You learned about *consonant to vowel linking* in Chapter 4. Link the last consonant sound to the first vowel sound of the next word.

Examples: give up   *sounds like* ⟶ gi-vup
   them all   *sounds like* ⟶ the-mall

Exercise 1 Say each phrase as if it were one word. Take turns with your partner.

Example: clean up ⟶ clea-nup

1. work out (v)   wor-kout
2. turn off (v)   tur-noff
3. back up (v)   ba-kup
4. log off (v)   lo-goff
5. Keep it.   Kee-pit.
6. What's up?   What-sup?
7. Hold on!   Hol-don!
8. Come in.   Co-min.
9. Let's eat.   Let-seat.
10. I opened it.   I open-dit

🎧 3, 40 Listen to your teacher or the speaker on the audio say each phrase two times. Then say each phrase two times *with* the teacher or the speaker.

Look at the list above. Choose two or three phrases you have said recently. Write them below. Write the situations. In groups of four, talk about your phrases.

Phrase   *Situation*

1. _____   _____

2. _____   _____

3. _____   _____

Exercise 2   There are "hidden" words in the lyrics to these songs. Link the words. Say the hidden word. Then say the lyrics.

Hidden word	♪ Lyrics ♫
Example: kick off, cough	Loose, footloose, kick off your Sunday shoes.
	From *Footloose*
1. feel it, lit	I feel it in my fingers, I feel it in my bones.
	From *Love is All Around*
2. ever after, rafter	Happy ever after in the market place.
	From *Ob la di*
3. mind I'm, dime	In my mind I'm goin' to Carolina.
	From *Carolina in my Mind*
4. life is, fizz	How wonderful life is while you're in the world.
	From *Your Song*
5. I'm all, mall	I'm in love, I'm all shook up.
	From *I'm All Shook Up*
6. All I, lie	All I ask is for you to come away with me.
	From *Come Away with me*
7. burned out, doubt	Your candle burned out long before your legend ever did.
	From *Candle in the Wind*
8. let her, letter	Remember to let her into your heart.
	From *Hey Jude*

Now *track* your teacher or the speakers on the audio as they say each line. *Tracking* is speaking *with* the speaker. Try to match linking, rhythm, pitch change, and speed.

Rule 14-1
What happens when we link two consonant sounds that are the same?

Examples: bla**ck c**offee

        o**ne n**ight

        weathe**r r**eport

☑ **The consonant sound is pronounced once, not twice. The sound is a little longer.**

Examples: I'll have bla**ck c**offee.

        He called o**ne n**ight last week.

        What's the weathe**r r**eport?

Exercise 3 Part A Close your eyes. Repeat the phrases in the box below after your teacher or the speaker on the audio. Use smooth linking.

bus stop	rock concert	fresh shrimp
speaks Spanish	wish she'd	Take care
watched TV	some more	ripe pears

Fill in the blanks with a phrase from the box and take turns reading the sentences. Say each phrase as if it were one word.

Example: My friend got us tickets to a <u>rock concert</u>.

1. Can you tell us where the closest _____ is?

2. I _____ be on time for a change.

3. Would you get a few _____ at the store?

4. Camilla _____ and Portuguese.

5. Last night I _____ and went to bed.

6. If you run out of paper, just ask Mark for _____.

7. _____ of yourselves.

8. I need a pound of _____.

Part B Practice "same consonant sound" linking (ro**ck c**oncert) and consonant-to-vowel linking (tel**l u**s). Listen to each phrase two times. Repeat it. Then say each sentence *with* the speaker two times.

Example: got us, rock concert

My friend got us tickets to a rock concert.

1. tell us, bus stop is
   Can you tell us where the bus stop is?

2. wish she'd
   I wish she'd be on time.

3. get a, ripe pears
   Would you get a few ripe pears?

4. speaks Spanish
   Camilla speaks Spanish.

5. watched TV, went to
   Last night I watched TV and went to bed.

6. run out of, some more
   If you run out of paper, Mark has some more.

7. take care
   Take care of yourselves.

8. need a, pound of, fresh shrimp
   I need a pound of fresh shrimp.

Something to Think About!

You learned that thought groups and pauses make you sound fluent. Linking does too. If you link words in a thought group, your speech will flow more smoothly.

Rule 14-2

Vowel-to-vowel linking. What sound is added to link these words? You will hear each phrase two times.

he isn't	*and*	stay in	⟶	/y/ or /w/?
too angry	*and*	go out	⟶	/y/ or /w/?

☑ **Some vowel sounds are linked by a /y/.**

he isn't   stay in   my answer
/y/   /y/   /y/

☑ **Other vowel sound are linked by a /w/.**

who isn't   go out   how are
/w/   /w/   /w/

Exercise 4 Say the phrases after the teacher or the speaker on the audio. Link the words smoothly. First read down, then across.

Add /y/	**Add /w/**
they owe /y/	you owe /w/
the ice cream /y/	no ice cream /w/
we ate /y/	who ate /w/
he always /y/	you always /w/
the end /y/	no end /w/
she agreed /y/	who agreed /w/

Exercise 5 Fill in the blanks with words from the box below. Write /y/ or /w/ under the links. Take turns reading the sentences.

Examples: I missed class yesterday.
        And it was extremely <u> important </u>.
                  /y/

        I missed class yesterday.
        And it was so <u> important </u>.
           /w/

important	ugly	unrealistic	unselfish
interesting	unhappy	upset	unhealthy
energetic	athletic	expensive	exciting

1. Nan's dream is to climb Mt. Everest.
   But he's not very _____.

2. My roommate painted his bedroom dark purple.
   It's so _____.

3. I'd love to spend a week in Paris.
   But it's too _____.

4. Last night we saw a movie about the Civil War.
   It was very _____.

5. Margareta's parents can't come for the holidays.
   She's really _____.

6. Chiaki takes classes, works, and volunteers at the homeless shelter.
   She is so _____.

7. Last night I ate a whole pint of cookie dough ice cream.
   It was delicious but really _____.

8. When I was in London, Gwyneth Paltrow got on an elevator with me.
   It was pretty _____.

Listen to the teacher or the speaker on the audio read the sentences.
[3, 47]

Rule 14-3

What happens when /t/ comes between vowels?

Examples: within a word: matter *sounds like* ⟶ ma**dd**er

between words: a lot of *sounds like* ⟶ a lo**dd**a

☑ **Before an unstressed syllable, the /t/ often sounds like a quick /d/ in North American English.**

It is not important to say /t/ as /d/ in words like *matter*. It is more important to recognize the sound change when you listen to English.

Cartoon copyrighted by Mark Parisi, printed with permission.

Listening Hint!

These words and phrases sound *almost* the same in North American English. Even native speakers depend on context!

Plato	Play-doh™
matter	madder
atom	Adam
great exams	grade exams

Exercise 6 Listen to the teacher or the speakers read the dialogues. The word in italics is what you *hear*. Cross it out and write the written form of the word.

Example: A: Hurry up. We're late.

             B: Could you please ~~waid~~ a minute? <u>wait</u>

1. A: Did you see Holly's engagement ring?
   B: Yeah. I *bed* it was expensive.   _____

2. A: Did you ever finish your degree?
   B: I finally *god* it.   _____

3. A: I'm late. I'm *meeding* Lin.   _____
   B: Okay. See you *lader*.   _____

4. A: It looks like rain.
   B: Yeah. You *bedder* take an umbrella.   _____

5. A: *Whad* do you need from the store?_____
   B: Just *ledduce and budder*.   _____ _____

6. A: She got an A on her composition.
   B: She's a good *rider*.   _____

Rule 14-4

3, 51

When /d/ is linked to /y/, what *new* sound is formed?

Example: /d/ + /y/: di**d** **y**ou

                       ma**de** **y**our

☑ **The /d/ + /y/ sounds like /ʤ/ as in *just*.**

di**d** **y**ou	=	di-ja
ma**de** **y**our	=	ma-jor

It is not necessary to say *di-ja* or *ma-jor*. It is more important to *hear* this sound change in the speech of others. If you practice *saying* the sound, however, you will become better at hearing it.

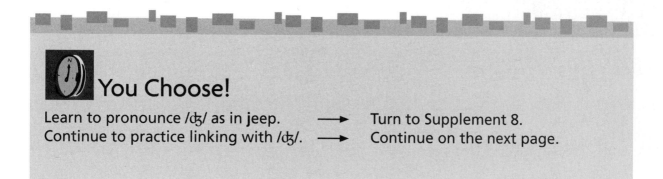

You Choose!

Learn to pronounce /ʤ/ as in jeep.   ⟶   Turn to Supplement 8.
Continue to practice linking with /ʤ/.   ⟶   Continue on the next page.

Exercise 7 Listen to the teacher or the speaker on the audio read the sentence in the present or past tense. Circle a. or b.

Example: a. They call you. *(present)*
(b.) They called you. *(past)*

1. a. They always play your favorite song.
   b. They always played your favorite song.

2. a. The police officers fine you.
   b. The police officers fined you.

3. a. We walk your dog every day.
   b. We walked your dog every day.

4. a. The students like your class.
   b. The students liked your class.

5. a. We owe you money.
   b. We owed you money.

Check your answers.
Now listen to both sentences in each pair. Repeat.

Communicative Practice ... asking questions and making requests

Take turns reading situations to your partner. *Student A:* See Box A. *Student B:* See Box B. Your partner should respond with a question or request that begins with a phrase in the box below.

Did you... j	*Should you...* j	*Would you mind...* j
Could you... j	*Would you...* j	

Example: A: You need to borrow a cell phone. What would you say?
j

B: Would you mind if I borrowed your cell phone for a minute.
j   j

What would you say?

Student A	Student B
Box A	Box B
1. You need to leave class early. What would you say to the teacher?	1. Request change for a dollar for the parking meter.
2. Request directions to the nearest ATM.	2. You didn't understand what someone just said to you.
3. The room is too warm. Ask if the thermostat can be turned down.	3. Your neighbor's stereo is loud. You can't sleep. Request that he turn it down.
4. The copy machine is broken. Ask the office assistant if he knew about the problem.	4. You will be a dinner guest at a friend's house. You want to know if it is a good idea to bring a hostess gift.
5. Your cell phone battery is dead. You need to borrow a cell phone.	5. Your friend just took her driving test. Ask if she got her license.

Pronunciation to Go!

What other questions do you have about being a dinner guest in someone's home? Write them here. Make links between words you will connect. Practice them with your partner in class.

Direct the questions to native speakers you know and trust. Report the answers to the class.

Example Question: _Should ‿ you ‿ arrive ‿ early, on time, or late?_

Example Answer: _For a dinner party, people usually arrive on time or_
about five minutes late.

Question 1: _Should you_ _____ ?

Answer 1: _____

_____

Question 2: _Should you_ _____ ?

Answer 2: _____

_____

Question 3: _Should you_ _____ ?

Answer 3: _____

_____

Consonant Supplements

Consonant Introduction

Supplement 1. Phonetic Alphabet

English words do not always sound the way they are written.

> These words have the same first letter—but different first sounds:
> *good* and *giraffe*

> These words have the same first sound—but different first letters:
> *send* and *city*

We use a special alphabet to show the sounds of the language. Each symbol represents a sound.

Most consonant symbols look like alphabet letters. Listen to the sounds and key words.

/p/	**p**ie	/f/	**f**ine	/l/	**l**et
/b/	**b**oy	/v/	**v**an	/r/	**r**ed
/t/	**t**en	/s/	**s**ee, ri**c**e	/w/	**w**e, **wh**ere, qui**z**
/d/	**d**ay	/z/	**z**oo, hi**s**	/y/	**y**es, **u**se
/k/	**k**ey, **c**old, du**ck**	/m/	**m**y	/h/	**h**ome
/g/	**g**o	/n/	**n**o		

Some consonant symbols do not look like alphabet letters.

/θ/	**th**ink
/ð/	**th**ey
/ʃ/	**sh**oe, na**ti**on
/ʒ/	mea**s**ure, vi**si**on, bei**g**e
/ʧ/	**ch**oose, na**tu**re
/ʤ/	**j**ob, **g**entle
/ŋ/	si**ng**, tha**n**k

Exercise 1 These are some of the most popular countries to visit. Write a country that begins with each sound listed below.

Japan	China	Canada	Poland
Thailand	Germany	Mexico	Greece
United States	Spain	France	Russia

Example: /p/ <u>Poland</u>

1. /k/ _____

2. /t/ _____

3. /tʃ/ _____

4. /y/ _____

5. /g/ _____

Check your answers.

Name a country you would most like to visit. _____
Does it begin with a consonant sound? If so, what sound? /   /

Exercise 2 These are some of the most popular first names in the United States and Canada. Find two names below that begin with each sound.

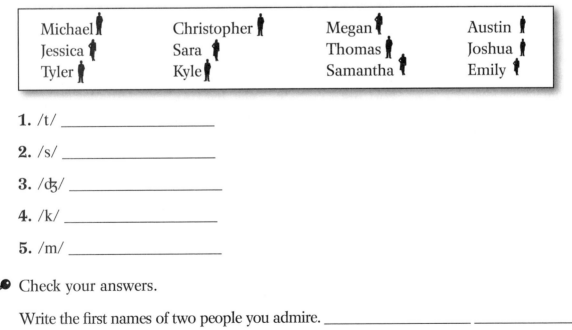

Michael	Christopher	Megan	Austin
Jessica	Sara	Thomas	Joshua
Tyler	Kyle	Samantha	Emily

1. /t/ _____

2. /s/ _____

3. /dʒ/ _____

4. /k/ _____

5. /m/ _____

Check your answers.

Write the first names of two people you admire. _____ _____
Do they begin with consonant sounds? If so, which ones? /   /   /   /

Supplement 2. Consonant Overview

We describe English consonant sounds in three ways. If you have trouble saying a sound, it is usually in one of these three ways.

Is the sound voiceless or voiced?

We make some consonant sounds *without* the voice. The sounds are **voiceless.** The vocal cords do not vibrate.

Put your hand on your throat. Make a snake-like hissing sound: s-s-s-s-s-s-s-s. There is no vibration.

An outlined letter is voiceless: s̸.

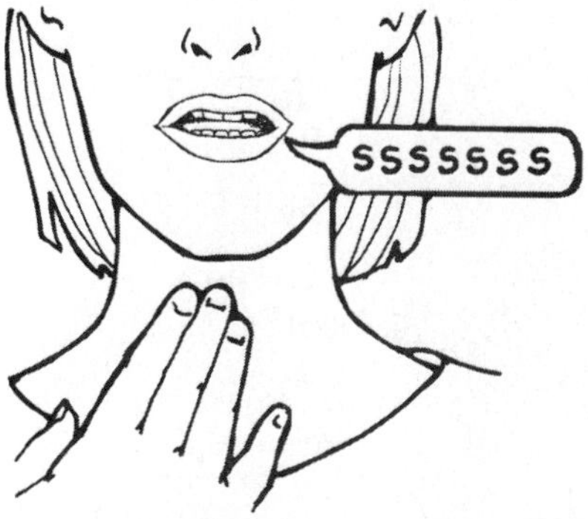

▲ Figure 1: SSSSSSSS No vibration of vocal cords.

We make other consonant sounds *with* the voice. They are **voiced.** The vocal cords vibrate.

Put your hand on your throat. Make a bee-like buzzing sound: z-z-z-z-z-z-z. Feel the vibration.

A letter with two vibrating lines is voiced: z̲.

▲ Figure 2: zzzzzzz Vibration of vocal cords.

English has eight consonant pairs that are almost alike. We say the sounds in each pair the same way—except that one is voiceless and the other is voiced.

Exercise 1 Listen to the teacher or the speaker say the word pairs. Listen to the difference between the voiceless and voiced sounds.

Voiceless		*Voiced*
1. /p/ pie	↔	/b/ buy
2. /t/ town	↔	/d/ down
3. /k/ cold	↔	/g/ gold
4. /f/ few	↔	/v/ view
5. /θ/ thank	↔	/ð/ they
6. /s/ sip	↔	/z/ zip
7. /ʃ/ ship	↔	/ʒ/ casual
8. /ʧ/ cheap	↔	/dʒ/ jeep

The rest of the consonant sounds are not paired. The /h/ in *hat* is voiceless. The /m/, /n/, /ŋ/, /r/, /l/, /w/, and /y/ are voiced.

Now *feel* the difference between the voiced and voiceless sounds. Put your hand on your throat. *Slowly* repeat the sound and word pairs above.

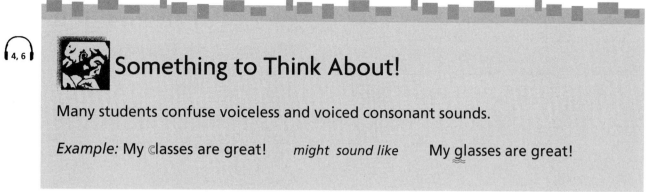

Something to Think About!

Many students confuse voiceless and voiced consonant sounds.

Example: My classes are great!   *might sound like*   My glasses are great!

Learn more about voiced and voiceless differences in Consonant Supplements 4 and 5.

How does the air move?

Say ffffffff. Say ssssssss. The air moves out of the mouth without stopping. Most consonant sounds like /f/ and /s/ continue without stopping. They are called **continuants.**

Say /p/. Say /t/. The air flow stops. Then it may be released. The air is stopped when we say these six sounds: /p/, /b/, /t/, /d/, /k/, and /g/. They are called **stops.**

Continuants
/s/ in le**ss**—The air flow continues

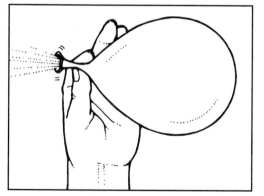

Stops
/t/ in le**t**—The air flow stops

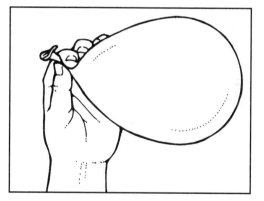

Exercise 2 Listen to the teacher or speaker say one of the words in each of the following pairs. Check (✓) the word you hear.

Examples: ___ less   ✓ let

         ✓ bus   ___ but

1. ___ boss   ___ bought

2. ___ bath   ___ bat

3. ___ both   ___ boat

4. ___ a nice manager   ___ a night manager

5. ___ the rice cereal   ___ the right cereal

6. ___ he's gone   ___ he'd gone

7. ___ lost his prize   ___ lost his pride

8. ___ which size   ___ which side

9. ___ he plays piano   ___ he played piano

10. ___ place setting   ___ plate setting

Check your answers.

Listen again. Now listen to the speaker say both words and phrases in each pair.

Something to Think About!

Students sometimes confuse continuants with stops.

Example: Would you pa**ss** the salt?   *might sound like*   Would you pa**t** the salt?

Where is the sound made?

What parts of the mouth stop the air or let small amounts of air pass through? What parts of the mouth touch or almost touch?

4, 10 Say /p/, /b/, and /m/. The lips close and stop the air. Say /w/. The lips are open and rounded. They let the air pass through.

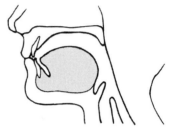

▲ **Figure 3:** Lips: / , , /

4, 11 Lightly bring the lower lip to the upper teeth. Force air through the light contact to say /f/. Add voice to say /v/.

▲ **Figure 4:** Lower lip and upper teeth: / , /

4, 12 Loosely touch the tip of the tongue against the back of the upper teeth. Move air through the loose contact to say /θ/ as in *thank*. Add voice to say /ð/ as in *they*.

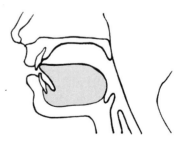

▲ **Figure 5:** Tip of tongue and back of upper teeth: /θ, ð/

Feel the gum area behind the upper teeth. To say /s/ and /z/, raise the tongue tip close to this gum ridge. To say /t, d, n, l/, firmly touch the tongue tip against the gum ridge.

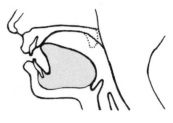

▲ Figure 6: Tip of tongue and gum ridge: / , , , /

Move your tongue past the gum ridge to the roof of the mouth—or palate. The front part is hard. To say /ʃ, ʒ, y, r/, part of the tongue is raised toward the hard palate.

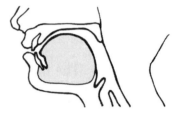

▲ Figure 7: Tongue and hard palate: / , , , ʒ/

The back of the palate is soft. Say /k/, /g/, and /ŋ/. Feel the back of the tongue touch the soft palate.

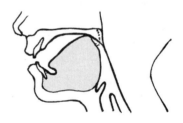

▲ Figure 8: Back of tongue and soft palate: / , g, ŋ/

Take a deep breath. Release the air. The sound made when you release the air is /h/. It is made in the glottis—the space between the vocal folds.

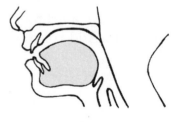

▲ Figure 9: Glottis: / /

Exercise 3 Repeat these common street names in the United States. Pay attention as you make each boldfaced sound. Circle the parts of your mouth that touch or almost touch.

Main • *Park* • *First* • *Fourth* • *Washington* • *Lake* • *Pine* • *Oak*

Example: **M**ain   (both lips)   lips-teeth   tongue-teeth

1. **P**ark	both lips	lips-teeth	tongue-teeth
2. **F**irst	both lips	lips-teeth	tongue-teeth
3. **W**ashington	both lips	lips-teeth	tongue-teeth
4. Four**th**	both lips	lips-teeth	tongue-teeth
5. **L**ake	tongue-gum ridge	tongue-hard palate	tongue-soft palate
6. Pi**n**e	tongue-gum ridge	tongue-hard palate	tongue-soft palate
7. Oa**k**	tongue-gum ridge	tongue-hard palate	tongue-soft palate

Check your answers.

What street do you live on? _____

Does it begin with a consonant sound? If so, which one? /   /

What parts of the mouth touch or almost touch? _____

Something to Think About!

Sometimes students are not sure where to put their tongue and lips to make consonant sounds.

     I have **gum** in my bag.   *might sound like*   I have **gun** in my bag.

Supplement 3. Selecting Consonant Sounds to Study

Problems with consonant sounds depend on the individual and her or his first language. The activities below will help you choose the sounds *you* need to practice.

Exercise 1 If a sound is not in your first language, it might be hard to hear. Listen to each set of phrases. Is it easy or hard to hear a difference? If hard, go to the supplement for more practice.

Example: /θ/ — /t/   it's **th**rough
it's **t**rue   ☐ Easy   ☐ Hard   ☞ *Supplement 7*

1. /θ/ — /s/   go to ma**th**
go to Ma**ss**   ☐ Easy   ☐ Hard   ☞ *Supplement 7*

2. /l/ — /r/   pi**l**ot software
pi**r**ate software   ☐ Easy   ☐ Hard   ☞ *Supplement 9*

3. /t/ — /d/   make the be**t**
make the be**d**   ☐ Easy   ☐ Hard   ☞ *Supplement 5*

4. /n/ — /m/   really do**n**e
really du**m**b   ☐ Easy   ☐ Hard   ☞ *Supplement 6*

5. /t/ — /d/   give me the **t**ime
give me the **d**ime   ☐ Easy   ☐ Hard   ☞ *Supplement 4*

6. /p/ — /b/   mail the **p**ills
mail the **b**ills   ☐ Easy   ☐ Hard   ☞ *Supplement 4*

7. /ʃ/ — /ʧ/   ca**sh** it
ca**tch** it   ☐ Easy   ☐ Hard   ☞ *Supplement 8*

8. /ʧ/ — /ʤ/   don't **ch**oke
don't **j**oke   ☐ Easy   ☐ Hard   ☞ *Supplement 8*

9. initial clusters   **p**ay it
play it   ☐ Easy   ☐ Hard   ☞ *Supplement 10*

10. final clusters   she's si**ck**
she's si**x**   ☐ Easy   ☐ Hard   ☞ *Supplement 11*

Exercise 2 Look at the Pronunciation Checklist in Chapter 1 on page 6. Did your teacher note consonant sounds that were difficult for you to say? What were they?

Consonant Practices

Supplement 4.

Initial	/p/	pie	–	/b/	buy
	/t/	time	–	/d/	dime
	/k/	cold	–	/g/	gold

All of these sounds are stops. When they are at the beginning of words, stop the air, then release it.

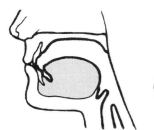

▲ **Figure 10** /p,b/

Stop the air at the lips.

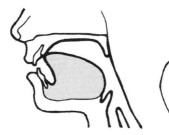

▲ **Figure 11** /t,d/

Stop the air where the tip of the tongue touches the gum ridge.

▲ **Figure 12** /k,g/

Stop the air where the back of the tongue touches the soft palate.

[4, 19] ☑ Release voiceless /p/, /t/, and /k/ with a puff of air—called *aspiration*—at the beginning of words.*

/p/	/t/	/k/
pill	time	kiss

If you do not use aspiration, /p/ will sound like /b/, /t/ will sound like /d/, and /k/ will sound like /g/.

He's **p**arking	*will sound like*	He's **b**arking
Could you give me the **t**ime?	*will sound like*	Could you give me the **d**ime?
Where's my **c**oat?	*will sound like*	Where's my **g**oat?

---

*Aspirate /p, t, k/ at the beginning of stressed syllables too: de**p**end, re**t**urn, re**c**ord (verb).

Listening Activity 1 Listen to the word pairs. Listen for aspiration with /p, t, k/.
Native speakers hear this clearly. You may need to listen carefully.

/p/–/b/	/t/–/d/	/k/–/g/
pack–back	time–dime	come–gum
peach–beach	tie–die	could–good
appear–a beer	tore–door	curl–girl

You will hear two words from the list above. If the words sound the same (*pack–pack*),
write __S__. If the words sound different (*pack–back*), write __D__.

1. _____   4. _____   7. _____

2. _____   5. _____   8. _____

3. _____   6. _____   9. _____

Check your answers.
Listen again. Now listen to both words in each pair.

Listening Activity 2 Listen to the teacher or the speaker on the audio say the prompt. Circle the correct answer.

	Prompt		*Answer*

1. ___ Did he catch the pass?   a. ___ Yes, and he made a touchdown.
   ___ Did he catch a bass (a fish)?   b. ___ Yes, and we had it for dinner.

2. ___ This is a huge pill.   a. ___ It's a vitamin.
   ___ This is a huge bill.   b. ___ It's from the hospital.

3. ___ Was it a good tip?   a. ___ More than 20 percent.
   ___ Was it a good dip?   b. ___ Delicious.

4. ___ Was it cold?   a. ___ No, warm and sunny.
   ___ Was it gold?   b. ___ No, silver.

Check your answers.
Listen again. Now listen to both prompts and responses.

Listening Activity 3 Listen to the paragraph. Listen again and fill in the blanks with words that have /p, t, k/ at the beginning.

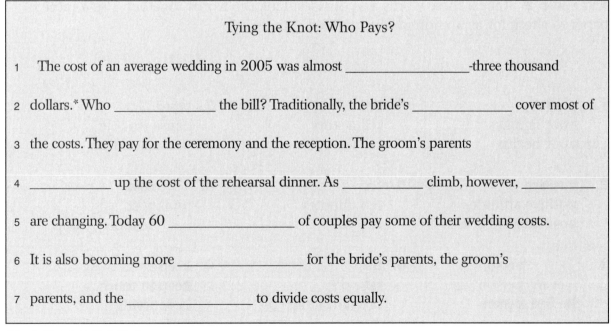

Tying the Knot: Who Pays?

1   The cost of an average wedding in 2005 was almost _____-three thousand

2   dollars.*Who _____ the bill? Traditionally, the bride's _____ cover most of

3   the costs. They pay for the ceremony and the reception. The groom's parents

4   _____ up the cost of the rehearsal dinner. As _____ climb, however, _____

5   are changing. Today 60 _____ of couples pay some of their wedding costs.

6   It is also becoming more _____ for the bride's parents, the groom's

7   parents, and the _____ to divide costs equally.

*Conde Nast Bridal Info Bank

Check your answers.

A Helpful Hint!

When you practice words with initial /p/, /t/ or /k/, hold a tissue or piece of paper in front of your mouth. The puff of air will make the tissue or paper move. You can also hold your hand in front of your mouth. You will feel the puff of air on your hand.

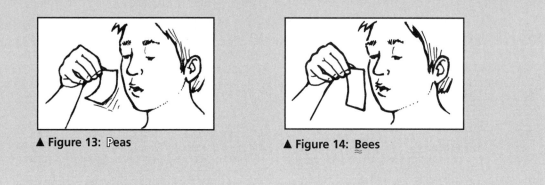

▲ Figure 13: Peas   ▲ Figure 14: Bees

Exercise 1 Repeat the word pairs in Listening Activity 1. Hold your hand in front of your mouth.

Exercise 2 Repeat these words and phrases. Link the words together. Use a piece of paper to check for aspiration on the outlined sounds.

/p/	/t/	/k/
1. poor poor families in poor health	**4.** tell tell a story tell the truth	**7.** cause cause trouble cause accidents
2. positive positive attitude positive feedback	**5.** ten ten minutes ten years	**8.** cost total cost cost per pound
3. person every person the first person	**6.** take take off take advantage of	**9.** keep keep in touch keep trying

Exercise 3 Repeat each prompt and answer in Listening Activity 3. Or, work with a partner.

> *Student A*: Check a prompt and say it to *Student B*.
> *Student B*: Check the answer and say it to *Student A*.

Check your answers, then switch roles.

Exercise 4 Find *Tying the Knot: Who Pays* in Listening Activity 3 in the Answer Key. Can you find more words with initial /p/, /t/, and /k/? Underline them. Read the paragraph chorally with your class or with the speakers until you can read it fluently.

Now record it. Listen to your pronunciation of the underlined words with /p/, /t/, and /k/. Repeat until you are satisfied with your recording.

Communicative Practice

Practice saying these items you might buy at the grocery store. Remember to say initial /p, t, k/ with aspiration.

tomato sauce	carrots	cake	paper towels
ketchup	pie	tea	pears
pepper	coffee	tuna fish	toilet tissue or paper

Which two items would you find in . . .

1. . . . the produce section? _____

2. . . . beverages? _____

3. . . . the bakery? _____

4. . . . spices and condiments? _____

5. . . . canned foods? _____

6. . . . paper products? _____

Small Group What other items that begin with /p/, /t/, or /k/ do you buy at the grocery store? Which group can make a list of the most items and say them correctly?

A Helpful Hint!

If someone misunderstands what you are saying, try to work out the misunderstanding. But, do not keep repeating the same thing over and over. Try these strategies:

1. Say it in other words.

Example: A: Can you *die* this for me?

B: *Dye* it? Color it?

A: No. You know, make a bow . . . *die* it.

B: Ah . . . *tie* it. Sure!

2. Give the topic or category.

Example: A: Do you want a *beach*?

B: What do you mean a *beach*?

A: I mean fruit—a *beach*.

B: I'd love a *peach*. Thanks!

3. Give more information.

Example: B: Where's David?

A: He went to *bet*.

B: He's at the casino?

A: No. He was tired. He went back to the hotel to sleep.

B: Oh, he went to *bed*.

Thanks to Eric Nelson for permission to adapt his pronunciation compensation strategies.

Supplement 5.

Final	/p/ cap	–	/b/ cab	
	/t/ seat	–	/d/ seed	
	/k/ back	–	/g/ bag	

When these stop consonant sounds occur at the *end* of words, the air may be released lightly. Sometimes the air is not released at all.

How do we tell /p/ from /b/, /t/ from /d/, and /k/ from/g/ at the end of words?

☑ Lengthen the vowel before the voiced stops /b/, /d/, and /g/.

Voiceless		*Voiced*
cap	↔	cab
lit	↔	lid
back	↔	bag

☑ Lengthen the vowel before other voiced consonants at the end of words too.

Voiceless		*Voiced*
leaf	↔	leave
bus	↔	buzz
rich	↔	ridge
		home
		pain

Listening Activity 1 Listen to the word pairs.

/p/–/b/	/t/–/d/	/k/–/g/
lap–lab	state–stayed	back–bag
cap–cab	debt–dead	dock–dog
rope–robe	feet–feed	lock–log

You will hear two words from the list above. If the words sound the same (*lap–lap*), write __S__. If the words sound different (*lap–lab*) , write __D__.

1. _____   4. _____   7. _____

2. _____   5. _____   8. _____

3. _____   6. _____   9. _____

🔑 Check your answers.
Listen again. Now listen to both words in each pair.

Listening Activity 2 Listen to the teacher or the speaker say the sentence. Fill in the blank with the letter or word.

/p/ or /b/

1. ___ Did you have any trouble finding a ca___?

2. ___ We're going to look for a pu___. Do you want to come?

3. ___ You didn't lose your notebook. It's in your la___.

/t/ or /d/

4. ___ She made the be___.

5. ___ I've lost the bea___.

6. ___ Louis fell off his bike and hurt his arm. I don't know if he can _____.
(write or ride)

/k/ or /g/

7. ___ Just put the coats in the ba___.

8. ___ That's not my pi___.

9. ___ We need to go to the hardware store for a lo___.

Check your answers.

Listening Activity 3 Listen to the paragraph. Listen again and fill in the blanks with words that have final /b/, /d/, and /g/.

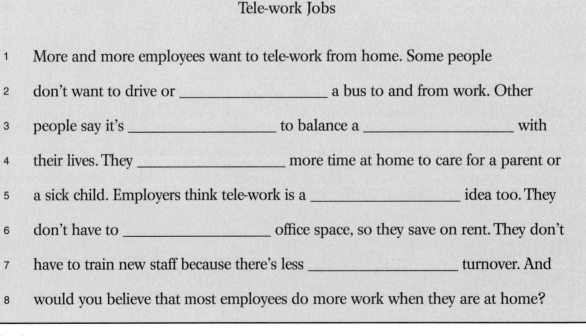

Tele-work Jobs

1   More and more employees want to tele-work from home. Some people

2   don't want to drive or _____ a bus to and from work. Other

3   people say it's _____ to balance a _____ with

4   their lives. They _____ more time at home to care for a parent or

5   a sick child. Employers think tele-work is a _____ idea too. They

6   don't have to _____ office space, so they save on rent. They don't

7   have to train new staff because there's less _____ turnover. And

8   would you believe that most employees do more work when they are at home?

Check your answers.

Exercise 1 **Exercise 1** Repeat the word pairs in Listening Activity 1. Lengthen the second word in each pair.

Exercise 2 Repeat the following words and phrases. Link the words together. If /b, d, g/ is the last sound in the phrase, release it lightly or not at all.

/b/	/d/	/g/
1. cab cab driver get a cab	**4.** need help need information need advice	**7.** bug bug spray caught a bug
2. web website world wide web	**5.** bed bed 'n breakfast going to bed	**8.** drug drug abuse drug addiction
3. job offered a job job training	**6.** bread loaf of bread fresh bread	**9.** bag sleeping bag plastic bag

Exercise 3 In Listening Activity 2, listen and repeat each sentence with both final sounds. Or work with a partner.

> *Student A*: Choose a sound to complete the sentence. Write it in the blank before the sentence. Dictate the sentence to your partner. *Student B*: Write the sentence on a piece of paper.

Take turns. Check your answers.

Exercise 4 Find *Tele-work Jobs* in Listening Activity 3 in the Answer Key. Read it chorally with your class or with the speakers until you can read it fluently.

Now record it. Listen to your pronunciation of the underlined words ending in /b/, /d/, and /g/. Repeat until you are satisfied with your recording.

Communicative Practice

Create a short story about the picture in the box. Try to use all the words.

Bob	bad
cab	drug
cold	good
red	

Tell your story to another pair.

Consonant Supplement Supplement 5 **165**

Supplement 6.

| /m/ some | – | /n/ sun | – | /ŋ/ sung |

Listening Activity 1 Listen to the three sounds.

/m/.../m/.../m/.../m/ and /n/.../n/.../n/.../n/ and /ŋ/.../ŋ/.../ŋ/.../ŋ/

Listening Activity 2 Listen to the word pairs.

/m/ vs. /n/	/m/ vs. /n/	/n/ vs. /ŋ/
some–son	dumb–done	sun–sung
comb–cone	same–sane	thin–thing
warm–warn	game–gain	win–wing

You will hear two words from the list above. If the words are the same (*some–some*), write __S__. If the words are different (*some–sun*), write __D__.

1. _____   4. _____   7. _____

2. _____   5. _____   8. _____

3. _____   6. _____   9. _____

 Check your answers.

Listen again. Listen to both words in each pair. Repeat the activity until you are confident of your answers.

Listening Activity 3 Listen to the teacher or the speaker on the audio say the prompt. Circle the correct answer.

Prompt   *Answer*

1. ___ Do you want a comb?   a. ___ Yes. My hair is a mess.
   ___ Do you want a cone?   b. ___ Yes. With a scoop of vanilla.

2. ___ What's the lime for?   a. ___ For your drink.
   ___ What's the line for?   b. ___ To tie up the boat.

3. ___ This is Tim.   a. ___ Hi Tim! Nice to meet you.
   ___ This is tin.   b. ___ We can't recycle it.

4. ___ Is he going to win it?   a. ___ His chances aren't good.
   ___ Is he going to wing* it?   b. ___ Yes. He has no time to prepare.

Check your answers.
Listen again. Now listen to both prompts and both answers.

_____

To wing it (informal expression) = to speak or act without preparation (e.g., He's going to wing his presentation).

Listening Activity 4 Listen to the paragraph. Fill in the blanks with words that end in /m/, /n/ and /ŋ/.

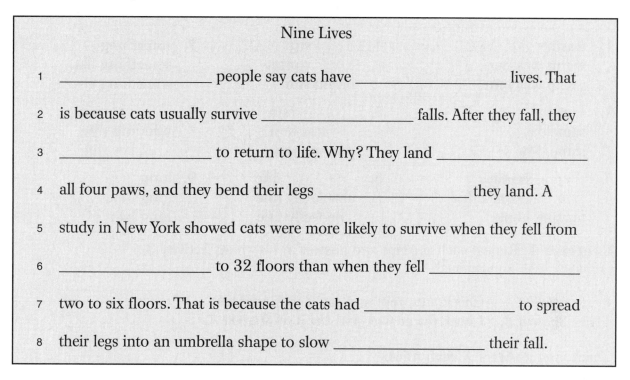

Nine Lives

1 _____ people say cats have _____ lives. That

2 is because cats usually survive _____ falls. After they fall, they

3 _____ to return to life. Why? They land _____

4 all four paws, and they bend their legs _____ they land. A

5 study in New York showed cats were more likely to survive when they fell from

6 _____ to 32 floors than when they fell _____

7 two to six floors. That is because the cats had _____ to spread

8 their legs into an umbrella shape to slow _____ their fall.

🔑 Check your answers.

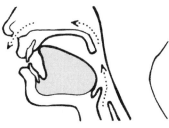

▲ **Figure 15:** /m/

The lips close. They keep the air from moving out of the mouth.

▲ **Figure 16:** /n/

The front part of the tongue touches the gum ridge and keeps the air from moving out of the mouth.

▲ **Figure 17:** /ŋ/

The back part of the tongue touches the soft palate and keeps the air from moving out of the mouth.

All three sounds are voiced.
All three sounds are nasal—the air flow is forced though the nose.

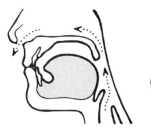 **Exercise 1** Repeat the sounds.

/m/. . ./m/. . ./m/. . ./m/   and   /n/. . ./n/. . ./n/. . ./n/   and   /ŋ/. . ./ŋ/. . ./ŋ/. . ./ŋ/

Exercise 2 Repeat the word pairs in Listening Activity 2.

Exercise 3 Repeat these words and phrases with /m/, /n/, and /ŋ/. Link the words together.

/m/	/n/	/ŋ/
1. warm warm weather warm welcome	**4.** sun sunset bright sun	**7.** something something like something else
2. same same day same time	**5.** rain acid rain pouring rain	**8.** ring wedding ring key ring
3. home home office nursing home	**6.** fine absolutely fine perfectly fine	**9.** long long time long hair

Exercise 4 Repeat each prompt and answer in Listening Activity 3. Or, work with a partner.

Student A: Check a prompt and say it to *Student B*.
Student B: Check the answer and say it to *Student A*.

Check your answers. Switch roles.

Exercise 5 Find *Nine Lives* in Listening Activity 4 in the Answer Key. Read it chorally with your class or with the speakers until you can read it fluently.

Now record it. Listen to your pronunciation of the underlined words with /m/, /n/, and /ŋ/. Repeat until you are satisfied with your recording.

Communicative Practice

Look at the information describing two vacations. Highlight the words with final /m/, /n/, and /ŋ/. Practice saying the words.

It is spring break. With your partner, decide which vacation you prefer. Why? Report your choice and your reasons to the class.

3-Day Spring Break Special
Ski/Snowboard

Canadian Rocky Lodge

- pool
- hot tub and steam room
- cable television, microwave oven, voicemail system, dataport, and iron in every room
- beautiful mountain views
- near downtown Banff

$99 per person* - U.S. dollars

*includes breakfast, ski lift voucher and bus transfer for all ski areas in Banff National Park

3-Day Sun and Fun Vacation
Ocean Front Inn

Soak up the sun, swim, spend quiet time in the warm dunes right outside your room.

- Florida's central east coast
- Affordable vacation haven
- Shopping, golfing, boating and other recreation nearby
- One hour drive from Orlando

*$99 per person
includes breakfast and airport shuttle

Choice: _____

Reason 1: _____

Reason 2: _____

Supplement 7.

/θ/   thin

 Listening Activity 1 Listen to each sound.

/θ/.../θ/.../θ and /s/.../s/.../s/ and /θ/.../θ/.../θ/ and /t/.../t/.../t/.../t/

 Listening Activity 2 Listen to the word pairs.

/θ/–/s/	/θ/–/t/	/θ/–/t/
think–sink	thank–tank	bath–bat
thing–sing	three–tree	both–boat
fourth–force	through–true	math–mat
mouth–mouse	thin–tin	tenth–tent

You will hear two words from the list above. If the words are the same (*think–think*), write __S__. If the words are different (*think–sink*), write __D__.

1. _____   4. _____   7. _____   10. _____
2. _____   5. _____   8. _____   11. _____
3. _____   6. _____   9. _____   12. _____

Check your answers.

Listen again. Listen to both words in each pair. Repeat the activity until you are confident of your answers.

 Listening Activity 3 Listen to the teacher or the speaker on the audio say the prompt. Circle the correct answer.

Prompt	*Answer*
1. ___ Is he the fif**th** one?	a. ___ No. The third one.
___ Is he the fi**t** one?	b. ___ No. He's out-of-shape.
2. ___ Bring your ma**th**.	a. ___ We can do homework.
___ Bring your ma**t**.	b. ___ We can do yoga.
3. ___ He has a big mou**th**.	a. ___ He can't keep a secret.
___ He has a big mou**se**.	b. ___ In his attic.
4. ___ It's **t**rue.	a. ___ Not false.
___ It's **th**rough.	b. ___ It's finished.

Check your answers.
Listen again. Now listen to both prompts and both answers.

Listening Activity 4 Listen to the paragraph. Listen again and fill in the blanks with words that have /θ/.

Earth Day

1   Each year we celebrate _____ Day, and _____ of school

2   children in Canada and the United States do what they can to protect and improve

3   the environment. One year students in Winnipeg started bringing trash-free

4   lunches to school every day. Now they _____ nothing away.

5   _____ grade students in Texas raised more than one _____

6   dollars at a garage sale. They used the money to protect twenty-_____

7   acres of rainforest in Costa Rica. And students in Pennsylvania made

8   _____ grocery bags for their parents to use year after year.

🔑 Check your answers.

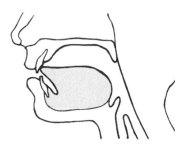

▲ Figure 18: /θ/

Loosely touch the tip of the tongue against the back of the upper teeth–near the cutting edge. The tongue is flat. Force air through the loose contact.

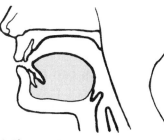

▲ Figure 19: /s/

Point the front of the tongue close to the tooth ridge. The front of the tongue is in a narrow v-shape. Force air down the V-shape groove.

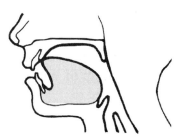

▲ Figure 20: /t/

Touch the tongue tip against the gum ridge. Stop the air flow.

All three sounds are voiceless.

Exercise 1 Repeat the sounds.

/θ/.../θ/.../θ/ and /s/.../s/.../s/ and /θ/.../θ/.../θ/ and /t/.../t/.../t/

Exercise 2 Repeat the word pairs in Listening Activity 2.

Exercise 3 Repeat these words and phrases with /θ/. Link the words together.

1. think
   think so
   think about it

2. three
   three o'clock
   three times

3. third
   third world
   third floor

4. fourth
   fourth grade
   fourth of July

5. thousand
   thousand pounds
   thousand dollars

6. Thursday
   Thursday night
   Thursday morning

7. method
   best method
   method of payment

8. faith
   great faith
   little faith

Exercise 4 Repeat each prompt and answer in Listening Activity 3. Or, work with a partner.

Student A: Check a prompt and say it to Student B.
Student B: Check the answer and say it to Student A.

Check your answers. Switch roles.

Exercise 5 Find *Earth Day* in Listening Activity 4 in the Answer Key. Read it chorally with your class or with the speakers until you can read it fluently.

Now record it. Listen to your pronunciation of the underlined words with /θ/. Repeat until you are satisfied with your recording.

Communicative Practice ... talk about dates and times

Look at your planners. *Student A:* Your planner is on this page.
Student B: Your planner is on page 212.

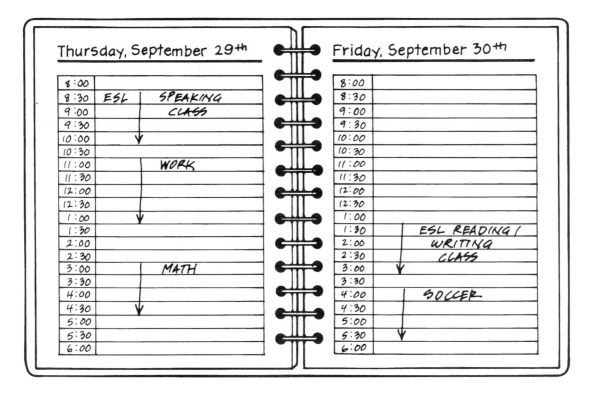

Call your partner. Find a time when you can get together to study and have coffee. You can change or rearrange your schedules. Don't let your partner see your planner.

Supplement 8.

/ʃ/ **sh**eep – /tʃ/ **ch**eap – /dʒ/ **j**eep

(5, 12) **Listening Activity 1** Listen to each sound.

/ʃ/.../ʃ/.../ʃ/.../ʃ/ and /tʃ/.../tʃ/.../tʃ/.../tʃ/ and /dʒ/.../dʒ/.../dʒ/.../dʒ/

(5, 13) **Listening Activity 2.** Listen to these word pairs.

/s/–/ʃ/	/t/–/tʃ/	/ʃ/–/tʃ/	/tʃ/–/dʒ/
see–she	tip–chip	she's–cheese	chin–gin
sue–shoe	too–chew	sheet–cheat	chose–Joe's
so–show	beat–beach	wish–which	choke–joke
seat–sheet	Pete–peach	wash–watch	rich–ridge

You will hear two words from the list above. If the words are the same (*she–she*), write ___*S*___. If the words are different (*see–she*), write ___*D*___.

1. _____	5. _____	9. _____	13. _____
2. _____	6. _____	10. _____	14. _____
3. _____	7. _____	11. _____	15. _____
4. _____	8. _____	12. _____	16. _____

Check your answers.

(5, 14) Listen again. Now listen to both words in each pair. Repeat the activity until you are confident of your answers.

(5, 15) **Listening Activity 3** Listen to the teacher or the speaker on the audio say the prompt. Circle the correct answer.

Prompt

1. ___ Did you get good **s**eats?
   ___ Did you get good **sh**eets?

2. ___ What're you wa**sh**ing?
   ___ What're you wa**tch**ing?

3. ___ Do you like that bea**t**?
   ___ Do you like that bea**ch**?

4. ___ Mar**ch** is almost here.
   ___ Mar**ge** is almost here.

5. ___ I think he was **j**oking.
   ___ I think he was **ch**oking.

Answer

a. ___ Yes, in the third row.
b. ___ Yes, 100 percent cotton.

a. ___ My car.
b. ___ Football.

a. ___ Yes. It's good for dancing.
b. ___ Yes. I go there on vacation a lot.

a. ___ Is it already the end of February?
b. ___ She just called on her cell phone.

a. ___ But nobody laughed.
b. ___ But he's fine now.

Check your answers.

(5, 16) Listen again. Now listen to both prompts and both answers.

Listening Activity 4 Listen to the paragraph. Listen again and fill in the blanks with
[5, 17] words that have /ʃ/, /tʃ/, and /dʒ/.

Short Vacations

1   Do you live to work or work to live? Many workers in the United States are asking

2   themselves that _____. Why? They get _____

3   vacations than workers in most other industrialized _____. The

4   average worker in the United States takes ten _____ days a year

5   after three years on the _____. U.S. law does not guarantee

6   workers any vacation time. _____ workers are guaranteed 15

7   vacation days. Workers in _____ are guaranteed ten days and take

8   an _____ of 18. _____ and _____

9   workers are guaranteed 25 paid vacation days and take an average of 30.

🔑 Check your answers.

🎧 Now listen to the answers from *Short Vacations*. Write them in the correct column.
[5, 18]

/ʃ/ as in sheep   /tʃ/ as in cheap   /dʒ/ as in jeep

_____   _____   _____

_____   _____   _____

_____   _____   _____

🔑 Check your answers.

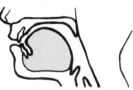

▲ **Figure 21:** /ʃ/

**Raise the front of the tongue to-
ward the hard palate. Round the
lips. Force air over the tongue. The
tongue is relaxed. /ʃ/ is voiceless.**

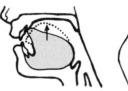

▲ **Figure 22:** /tʃ/

**Stop the air completely by
making a stop /t/. Then open
into an /ʃ/ sound.**

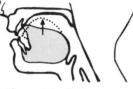

▲ **Figure 23:** /dʒ/

**Make the /dʒ/ exactly like the /tʃ/
except add voice.**

Exercise 1 Repeat the sounds.
[5, 19]

/ʃ/ . . . /ʃ/ . . . /ʃ/ . . . /ʃ/   and   /tʃ/ . . . /tʃ/ . . . /tʃ/ . . . /tʃ/   and   /dʒ/ . . . /dʒ/ . . . /dʒ/ . . . /dʒ/

Exercise 2 Repeat the word pairs in Listening Activity 2.
[5, 20]

Note: /ʒ/ as in *vision, measure, beige, decision,* and *explosion* is made the same way as /ʃ/ but with voice. /ʒ/ is not as common a
sound in English.

A Helpful Hint!

What is the difference in meaning between these sentences?

> They're going to <u>change mail</u> addresses.
> They're going to <u>change e-mail</u> addresses.

> The article's on <u>page 12</u>.
> The article's on <u>page E-12</u>.

Be careful not to add /iʸ/ to all words that end in /ʃ/, /tʃ/ and /dʒ/. For example, say *page* (not *page-ee*), *language* (not *language-ee*) and *match* (not *match-ee*). If you add a sound, you might change the meaning.

 Exercise 3 Repeat these words and phrases with /ʃ/, /tʃ/ and /dʒ/.
5, 21

/ʃ/	/tʃ/	/dʒ/
1. should	**5. ch**ild	**9.** June
should go	**ch**ild care	mid June
should be able	**ch**ild support	June wedding
2. **sh**ow	**6.** **ch**ange	**10.** July
TV **sh**ow	address **ch**ange	end of July
talk **sh**ow	political **ch**ange	4th of July
3. share	**7. ch**oose	**11. ch**ange
share ideas	**ch**oose between	chan**ge** the subject
share blame	**ch**oose whichever	chan**ge** your mind
4. **sh**ation	**8.** Fren**ch**	**12.** a**ge**
radio **sh**ation	Fren**ch** language	school a**ge**
gas **sh**ation	fren**ch** fries	middle a**ge**

Exercise 4 Repeat each prompt and answer in Listening Activity 3.
5, 22 Or, work with a partner.

> *Student A*: Check a prompt and say it to *Student B*.
> *Student B*: Check the answer and say it to *Student A*.

Check your answers. Switch roles.

Exercise 5 Find *Short Vacations* in Listening Activity 4 in the Answer Key. Repeat the words in the lists below the paragraph. Read the paragraph chorally with your class or with the speakers until you can read it fluently.

Then record it. Listen to your pronunciation of the underlined words with /ʃ/, /ʧ/, and /ʤ/. Repeat until you are satisfied with your recording.

Communicative Practice . . . choosing a flavor

Take turns ordering at this ice cream parlor. Include number of scoops, flavors, and cone or dish. If you want a shake, what flavor do you want?

Famous HOMEMADE ICE CREAM	DELICIOUS SHAKES
Dish or fresh waffle cone!	Any flavor!

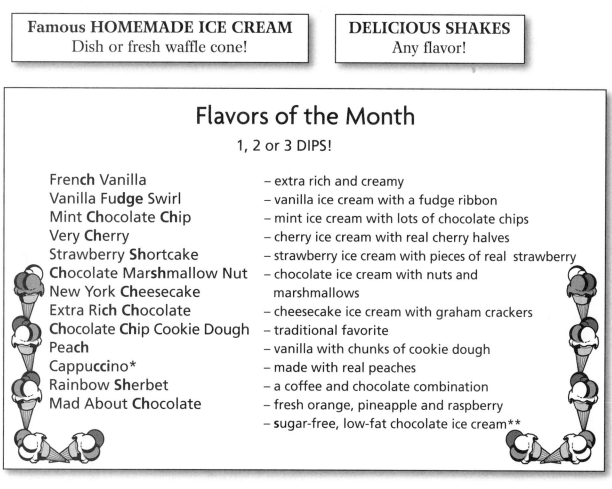

Flavors of the Month

1, 2 or 3 DIPS!

Fren**ch** Vanilla — extra rich and creamy
Vanilla Fu**dge** Swirl — vanilla ice cream with a fudge ribbon
Mint **Ch**ocolate **Ch**ip — mint ice cream with lots of chocolate chips
Very **Ch**erry — cherry ice cream with real cherry halves
Strawberry **Sh**ortcake — strawberry ice cream with pieces of real strawberry
Chocolate Mar**sh**mallow Nut — chocolate ice cream with nuts and marshmallows
New York **Ch**eesecake — cheesecake ice cream with graham crackers
Extra Ri**ch Ch**ocolate — traditional favorite
Chocolate **Ch**ip Cookie Dough — vanilla with chunks of cookie dough
Pea**ch** — made with real peaches
Cappu**cc**ino* — a coffee and chocolate combination
Rainbow **Sh**erbet — fresh orange, pineapple and raspberry
Mad About **Ch**ocolate — **s**ugar-free, low-fat chocolate ice cream**

*The cc- in cappuccino = /ʧ/.   **The *s*- in **s**ugar = /ʃ/.

What are the three most popular flavors in your group? Report them to the class.

1. _____   2. _____   3. _____

Supplement 9.

/l/   light   –   /r/   right

Listening Activity 1 Listen to each sound.

/l/.../l/.../l/.../l/.../l/   and   /r/.../r/.../r/.../r/.../r/

Listening Activity 2 Listen to the word pairs.

/l/–/r/		
light–right	lock–rock	collect–correct
long–wrong	long–wrong	pilot–pirate
lead–read	lap–rap	tile–tire

You will hear two words from the list above. If the words are the same (*light–light*), write ___S___. If the words are different (*light–right*), write ___D___.

1. _____   4. _____   7. _____

2. _____   5. _____   8. _____

3. _____   6. _____   9. _____

Check your answers.
Listen again. Listen to both words in each pair. Repeat the activity until you are confident of your answers.

Listening Activity 3 Listen to the teacher or the speaker on the audio say the prompt. Circle the correct answer.

	Prompt		*Answer*
1.	___ Is it long?	a.	___ No. It's short.
	___ Is it wrong?	b.	___ No. It's right.
2.	___ Is it light?	a.	___ No. It's still dark.
	___ Is it right?	b.	___ No. It's wrong.
3.	___ Was he a pilot?	a.	___
	___ Was he a pirate?	b.	___
4.	___ I need rocks.	a.	___ For the garden?
	___ I need locks.	b.	___ For the doors?

Check your answers.
Listen again. Now listen to both prompts and both answers.

Listening Activity 4 Listen to the paragraph. Listen again and fill in the blanks with words that have /l/ and /r/.

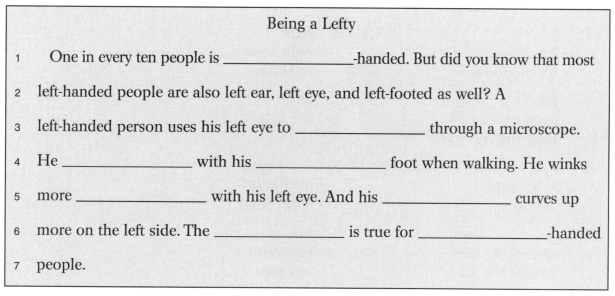

Being a Lefty

1   One in every ten people is _____-handed. But did you know that most

2 left-handed people are also left ear, left eye, and left-footed as well? A

3 left-handed person uses his left eye to _____ through a microscope.

4 He _____ with his _____ foot when walking. He winks

5 more _____ with his left eye. And his _____ curves up

6 more on the left side. The _____ is true for _____-handed

7 people.

🔑 Check your answers.

▲ **Figure 24** /l/

▲ **Figure 25** /r/

▲ **Figure 26** /l/

Imagine you are holding a piece of candy on the gum ridge with just the tip of your tongue. Direct the air around the sides of the tongue.

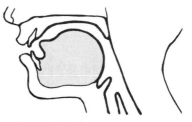

▲ **Figure 27** /r/

The tip of the tongue points to the roof of the mouth but does NOT touch it. The sides of the tongue touch the upper back teeth. Lips are slightly rounded. Air flows over the center of the tongue.

Exercise 1 Repeat the sounds.

/l/ . . . / l/ . . . / l/ . . . / l/ . . . / l/   and   /r/ . . . / r/ . . . / r/ . . . / r/ . . . / r/

Exercise 2 Repeat the word pairs in Listening Activity 2.

Exercise 3 Repeat these words and phrases with /l/ and /r/. Link the words together.

	/l/		/r/
1.	lot	**5.**	right
	a **lot** of time		**right** now
	a **lot** of money		**right** here
2.	legal	**6.**	red
	legal advice		**red** hair
	legal rights		**red** meat
3.	love	**7.**	road
	love songs		main **road**
	love story		dirt **road**
4.	land	**8.**	rap
	owned the **land**		**rap** music
	bought the **land**		**rap** star

Exercise 4 Repeat each prompt and answer in Listening Activity 3. Or, work with a partner.

> *Student A*: Check a prompt and say it to *Student B*.
> *Student B*: Check the answer and say it to *Student A*.

Check your answers. Switch roles.

Exercise 5 Find *Being a Lefty* in Listening Activity 4 in the Answer Key. Find more words that begin with /l/ and /r/. Underline them. Read the paragraph chorally with your class or with the speakers until you can read it fluently.

Now record it. Listen to your pronunciation of the underlined words with /l/ and /r/. Repeat until you are satisfied with your recording.

Communicative Practice

Create a story about the picture in the box. Try to use all the words with /r/ and /l/.

late
alone
flat
road
tire
Rob's
  Towing
  Service

Tell your story to another pair.

Supplement 10. Initial Consonant Clusters

English words can have two or three consonant sounds at the beginning:

2 consonant sounds:	/sp/	spell	/gr/	green
3 consonant sounds:	/str/	strange	/spr/	spring

In this supplement, you will practice initial clusters with two consonant sounds.

Listening Activity 1 Circle the word you hear in each pair.

[5, 35]

> *Example:* so–slow
>
> pace–place   box–blocks   state–estate
> say–stay   fee–free   train–to rain
> back–black   sell–smell   slow–so low

Check your answers.

[5, 36] Listen again. Listen to both words and phrases in each pair.

Initial Consonant Cluster Rule 1

[5, 37] Never *omit* a consonant sound in an initial cluster. You might change the meaning.

Examples:	play	→	pay
	free	→	fee

Initial Consonant Cluster Rule 2

[5, 38] Do not *add* a vowel sound before the consonants or between the consonants. You might change the meaning.

Examples:	dress	→	address	*Examples:*	trip	→	to rip
	state	→	estate		sport	→	support

Exercise 1 Make new words. Fill in the blank with a consonant sound from the box.

Example: s_t_ore

1. b __ ake
2. p __ ay
3. g __ ass
4. b __ ow
5. s __ it
6. s __ ay
7. b __ ack
8. s __ end
9. t __ ip
10. s __ ack

/r/

/l/

/p/

/t/

/n/

Check your answers.
Repeat the words in the Answer Key.

5, 39

If the first consonant is a *continuant*, continue it to the next consonant sound.

Examples:　ssstay
　　　　　　sssnack (remember /s/ is voiceless)

If the first consonant is a *stop*, do not release it until you are ready to say the next consonant sound.

Examples:　blow (release /b/ as you say /l/)
　　　　　　trip (release /t/ as you say /r/)

Exercise 2 Listen to the teacher or the speaker on the audio say each sentence. Did the speaker say the consonant cluster? Check *Yes* or *No*.

	Yes 👍	No 👎
Example: I'd like more please.	__ please	✓ peas
1. This bread is hard.	__ bread	__ bed
2. Did you see my new plants?	__ plants	__ pants
3. That tire looks flat.	__ flat	__ fat
4. He'll break her heart.	__ break	__ bake
5. Let's take the freeway.	__ freeway	__ feeway
6. Can you smell the cookies?	__ smell	__ sell
7. She has a small plane.	__ plane	__ pain
8. Can you hear the wind blow?	__ blow	__ below
9. He plays lots of sports.	__ sports	__ supports
10. I have a twin sister.	__ twin	__ to win

Check your answers.
Listen again. Repeat each sentence as written.

Communicative Practice . . . resolutions

Resolutions are personal goals for the year ahead. Below are some common New Year's resolutions. Practice the words with initial consonant clusters.

Then identify resolutions you want to make in the coming years. Talk about them with your partner.

Drop (lose) ten pounds	Clean out closets and drawers
Stop smoking	Try to be more patient
Start exercising	Stop watching so much TV
Stick to a budget	Spend less time online
Start a new hobby	Start college
Graduate from college	Learn a new skill
Others:_____	
_____	

Supplement 11. Final Consonant Clusters

Many English words have two consonant sounds at the end.

    2 consonant sounds: fa<u>st</u> /st/   ki<u>nd</u> /nd/   mo<u>ves</u> /vz/

English words also have three consonant sounds at the end. Most of these words have an -*s* or an -*ed* ending.

    3 consonant sounds: wo<u>rks</u> /rks/   fo<u>rced</u> /rst/   pri<u>nts</u> /nts/

In this section, you will practice two-consonant clusters and a few three-consonant clusters at the end of words.

Listening Activity 1 Circle the word you hear in each pair.

Example: (fine)–find

wait–waist	sing–sink	fell–felt
stop–stopped	need–needs	car–card
fat–fact	nice–nights	mint–minute
sin–since	mine–mind	scalp– scallop

Listen again. Listen to both words and phrases in each pair.

Exercise 1 Make new words. Fill in the blanks with a consonant sound from the box below. Say the words.

/s/	/t/	/d/	/l/

Example: be <u>l</u> t   be <u>s</u> t

1. ten___   ten___   ten___

2. fa___t

3. wai___t

4. take___

5. save___   save___

6. love___   love___

Check your answers.
Repeat the words after the teacher or speaker on the audio.

Make final clusters easier to say.

Final Consonant Cluster Rule

If the next word in the phrase begins with a vowel, move the last consonant to the next word.

Examples: /dz/ He can use my car / if he nee<u>ds</u> it. (if he need <u>z</u>it)

/kt/ The fa<u>ct</u> is / I ran out of money. (the fak <u>t</u>is)

Exercise 1 Repeat the words and phrases after the teacher or speaker on the audio.

	Word		*Link to a Vowel*	
1.	fa<u>st</u>	/st/	fa<u>st</u> asleep	(fas tasleep)
2.	co<u>ld</u>	/ld/	co<u>ld</u> air	(col dair)
3.	ne<u>xt</u>	/kst/	ne<u>xt</u> election	(neks telection)
4.	si<u>nce</u>	/ns/	si<u>nce</u> April	(sin sapril)
5.	ta<u>kes</u>	/ks/	ta<u>kes</u> effort	(take seffort)
6.	nee<u>ds</u>	/dz/	nee<u>ds</u> our help	(need zour help)
7.	toa<u>st</u>	/st/	toa<u>st</u> and jam	(toas tand jam)
8.	ligh<u>ts</u>	/ts/	ligh<u>ts</u> out	(light sout)

Note: In final clusters with *three* consonants, native speakers often omit the middle sound when it is a /t/ or /d/. *Examples: fac̶ts, han̶ds.* The next level of *Well Said* provides more practice with three consonant clusters.

Exercise 2 Listen to the teacher or the speaker on the audio say each sentence. Did the speaker say the consonant cluster? Check *Yes* or *No*.

	Yes 👍	No 👎
Example: The police will fi<u>nd</u> him.	✔ find	__ fine
1. She got a ca<u>rd</u> on her birthday.	__ card	__ car
2. They wa<u>lked</u> every morning.	__ walked	__ walk
3. They showed me where they wo<u>rk</u>.	__ work	__ were
4. Did you get new pa<u>nts</u>?	__ pants	__ pans
5. I'm calling about the a<u>nts</u> in my room.	__ ants	__ ant
6. That's a fa<u>ct</u>.	__ fact	__ fat
7. Are you fini<u>shed</u>?	__ finished	__ Finnish
8. Would you make the be<u>ds</u>?	__ beds	__ bed
9. They he<u>lped</u> him pay the rent.	__ helped	__ help
10. He has a bea<u>rd</u>.	__ beard	__ beer

🔑 Check your answers.

Listen again. Repeat each sentence as written.

Communicative Practice . . . What do you fear?

Here are some common phobias–strong fears or dislikes. Can you think of any more? Write them in the box below.

Do you have any of these fears? Take a survey. Find out the most common phobias in your group. Tell your group a story about how your phobia has affected your life. Pay attention to final clusters. Review initial clusters (e.g., *flying*, *snakes*, *spiders*).

sha<u>rks</u>	/rks/	flying in pla<u>nes</u>	/nz/
tall buildi<u>ngs</u>	/ŋz/	sna<u>kes</u>	/ks/
elevato<u>rs</u>	/rz/	spide<u>rs</u> and bugs	/rz/ /gz/
the da<u>rk</u>	/rk/	compute<u>rs</u>	/rz/
Others:_____			

Vowel Supplements

Vowel Introduction

Supplement 12. Phonetic Alphabet

English words do not always sound the way they are written.

These words have the same vowel letters—but different vowel sounds.

c<u>a</u>t   f<u>a</u>ther   <u>a</u>bout

These words have different vowel letters—but the same vowel sound.

n<u>a</u>m<u>e</u>   d<u>ay</u>   <u>ei</u>ght

We use a special alphabet to show the vowel sounds of English.

Each vowel sound has a symbol and a key word.
Listen to the fifteen sounds and key words.

Vowel 1. /i^y/ he	Vowel 6. /ɜr/ b**ir**d	Vowel 9. /u^w/ too
Vowel 2. /ɪ/ hit	Vowel 7. /ʌ/ cup	Vowel 10. /ʊ/ **goo**d
Vowel 3. /e^y/ may	/ə/ **a**bout (unstressed)	Vowel 11. /o^w/ no
Vowel 4. /ɛ/ get	Vowel 8. /ɑ/ hot	Vowel 12. /ɔ/ law
Vowel 5. /æ/ mad		Vowel 13. /aɪ/ fine
		Vowel 14. /aʊ/ n**ow**
		Vowel 15. /ɔɪ/ b**oy**

Exercise 1 Write the number of the vowel sound above each word in the box. For example, the vowel sound in *blue* is Vowel 9: /u^w/ as in *too*.

Example: blue ⁹	pink	green	white	gray
brown	red	black	p<u>ur</u>ple	

Check your answers.

Supplement 13. Vowel Overview

Say *ah* (Vowel 8 as in *hot*). Say *oh* (Vowel 11 as in *no*).
When we say vowel sounds, the air flows freely. We do not block the air with the lips, teeth, or tongue. We make different vowel sounds by changing the size and shape of the mouth.

Exercise 1 Circle the answer. The first one is done for you.

1. a. Say /iʸ/ as in *he*.
The tongue bunches up in the (front of the mouth), back of the mouth).

b. Say /uʷ/ as in *too*.
The tongue bunches up in the (front of the mouth, back of the mouth).

2. a. Put your fingers on the sides of your mouth. Say /iʸ/ as in *he*.
The lips are (spread, rounded).

b. Put your fingers on the sides of your mouth. Say /uʷ/ as in *too*.
The lips are (spread, rounded).

3. a. Put your hand on your chin. Say /ɑ/ as in *hot*.
The jaw and the tongue are (high, low).

b. Put your hand on your chin. Say /iʸ/ as in *he*.
The jaw and the tongue are (high, low).

🔑 Check your answers.

We describe vowel sounds by the position of the tongue, lips, and jaw.

Front Vowels

The front of the tongue starts high in the mouth. The tongue and jaw move down as you say the front vowels. The lips are spread.

🎧 6, 2 Look at Figure 28. Listen and repeat the front vowels: /iʸ, ɪ, eʸ, ɛ, æ/. Now listen and repeat the sounds and words below.

Vowel 1. /iʸ/   he, these, leaf, feed, _____
Vowel 2. /ɪ/   hit, sick, win, miss, pin, _____
Vowel 3. /eʸ/   may, rain, paint, late, same, _____
Vowel 4. /ɛ/   get, yes, red, jet, send, _____
Vowel 5. /æ/   mad, sad, man, bag, pan, _____

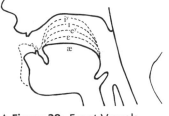

▲ **Figure 28:** Front Vowels

Exercise 2 Write these words in the blanks above: men, hat, sit, cheese, wait.

🔑 Check your answers.

Back Vowels

The back of the tongue starts high in the mouth. As you say the back vowels, the tongue and jaw move down. The lips are rounded.

6, 3 Look at Figure 29. Listen and repeat the back vowels: /uʷ, ʊ, oʷ, ɔ/. Now listen and repeat the sounds and words below.

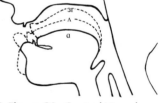

Vowel 9. /uʷ/ too, food, choose, rule, suit, _____
Vowel 10. /ʊ/ good, book, pull, full, should, _____
Vowel 11. /oʷ/ know, soap, home, joke, phone, _____
Vowel 12. /ɔ/ law, long, ball, caught, walk, _____

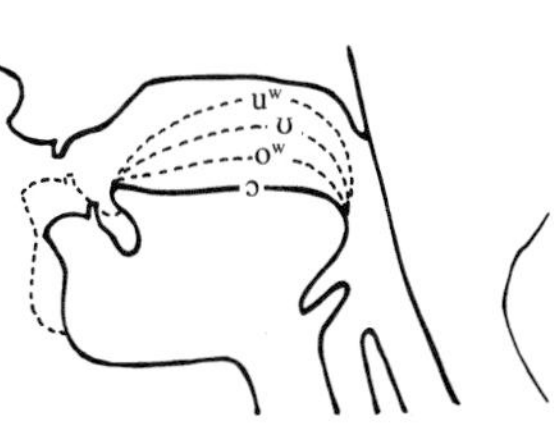

▲ **Figure 29:** Back Vowels

Exercise 3 Write these words in the blanks above: boss, close, moon, could.

Check your answers.

Central Vowels

As you say the central vowels, the tongue starts high and moves down. For vowels 7 and 8, the lips are in a neutral position. They are not spread or rounded.

6, 4 Look at Figure 30. Listen and repeat the back vowels: /ɜr, ʌ, ə, ɑ/. Now listen and repeat the sounds and words below.

Vowel 6. /ɜr/ bird, her, nurse, work, _____
Vowel 7. /ʌ/ cup, truck, gum, run, _____
/ə/* a̲bout, sof a̲, a, the, _____
Vowel 8. /ɑ/ hot, stop, job, shop, _____

▲ **Figure 30:** Central Vowels

Exercise 4 Write these words in the blanks above: hurt, A̲merica̲, socks, bug.

Check your answers.

_____

*The /ə/ or schwa occurs in unstressed syllables and words. The /ʌ/ occurs in stressed syllables and words. *Example:* aBOVE = /əbʌv/.

Diphthongs

Diphthongs combine two full vowel sounds. The first vowel sound starts low in the mouth. The tongue moves to a second, much higher vowel sound.

🎧 6, 5 Listen and repeat.

Vowel 13. /aɪ/ fine, white, light, sky, tie, _____

Vowel 14. /aʊ/ now, house, south, brown, _____

Vowel 15. /ɔɪ/ boy, toy, noise, join, _____

Exercise 5 Write these words in the blanks above: loud, boil, drive.

🔑 Check your answers.

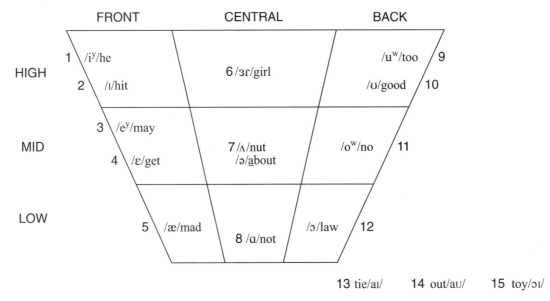

▲ **Figure 31:** The Vowel Chart showing the vowels of North American English

Exercise 6 The most important vowel sound in a word is the vowel sound with the main stress. Write the number of the vowel sound above the stressed syllable.

Example: beGIN
(2)

1. conFUSE   4. NoVEMber

2. JaPAN   5. fourTEEN

3. DIRty

🔑 Check your answers.

🎧 6, 6 Listen and repeat the words. Make the stressed vowels full and clear.

Exercise 7 Unstressed vowels often sound like the schwa sound /ə/ as in _about_. Write /ə/ over _unstressed_ vowels that sound like schwa. The teacher or speaker will say each word twice.

ə   ə

Example: de VEL op

1. oc CUR

2. a LONE

3. POS si ble

4. com PARE

5. tra DI tion

Check your answers.

Listen and repeat the words. Keep the /ə/ in the background. Imagine that it is humble and shy and does not want to stand out.

Exercise 8 The most important vowel sound in a phrase is the one in the focus word (or syllable). Write the number of the vowel sound over each focus word in the dialogue. The first one is done for you.

5

A: What's the **MAT**ter?

B: I don't know what to wear to **SCHOOL**.

A: Just throw on jeans and a **SHIRT**.

B: But **WHICH** shirt?

A: Your **TEE** shirt.

B: My **BLUE** tee shirt, my **BLACK** tee shirt, my **TIE** dye tee shirt, **CON**cert tee shirt, **BASE**ball tee shirt . . . ?

A: Just get **DRESSED**! We're gonna be **LATE**!

Check your answers.

Listen and repeat the dialogue. Or practice the dialogue with your partner.

Simple and Glided Vowels

Eight vowel sounds are called *simple* or *pure* vowels. They have only one sound from beginning to end. That is why they have only one symbol (except for /ɜr/).

Four vowel sounds are not simple. They glide or move toward a second sound. That is why they have a second symbol—/ʸ/ or /ʷ/.

Simple	Glided
/ɪ/	/iʸ/
/ɛ/	/eʸ/
/ʊ/	/uʷ/
/ɔ/	/oʷ/
/æ/	
/ɜr/	
/ʌ/	
/ɑ/	

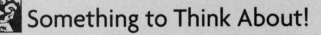

Something to Think About!

Students often confuse glided and simple vowels.

Example: /iʸ/ She's l<u>ea</u>ving there.   *might sound like*   /ɪ/ She's l<u>i</u>ving there.
/eʸ/ I need some p<u>a</u>per.   *might sound like*   /ɛ/ I need some p<u>e</u>pper.

Exercise 9 Listen to the teacher or the speaker on the audio say the sound pairs.

Simple		Glided
/ɪ/	⟶	/iʸ/
/ɛ/	⟶	/eʸ/
/ʊ/	⟶	/uʷ/
/ɔ/	⟶	/oʷ/

Now listen to the teacher or speaker *whisper* the sound pairs. Was it easier to hear the difference?

Exercise 10 Read your teacher's *lips* as your teacher silently says the sound pairs. Can you *see* the difference between the glided and the simple vowels?

Your teacher will say a sound from Column 1 or 2. Hold up one finger or two fingers to show which column the sound is from.

1. No Movement   2. Movement

/ɪ/   ⟶   /iʸ/
/ɛ/   ⟶   /eʸ/
/ʊ/   ⟶   /uʷ/
/ɔ/   ⟶   /oʷ/

You will learn more about the first three sound pairs in Supplements 15, 16, and 17.

A Helpful Hint!

When you see two vowels in a one-syllable word, the first vowel is often pronounced like the letter name. The second vowel is silent.

rain	name	may	=	A or /eʸ/
meat	feel		=	E or /iʸ/
pie	mine		=	I or /aɪ/
boat	home	know	=	O or /oʷ/
use	cute		=	U or /yuʷ/*

*Note: The *-ue* as in *blue* and *due* and *-u-e* as in *June* and *rule* are usually pronounced /uʷ/ without the /y/.

Exercise 11 Write each phrase in the blanks under the correct vowel sound. The first one is done for you.

late date	true blue	slow boat	bike ride
arrive alive	same page	gray day	cream cheese
clean jeans	sea breeze	green tea	nice smile

A or /eʸ/	E or /iʸ/	I or /aɪ/	O or /oʷ/	/ uʷ/
late date	_____	_____	_____	_____
_____	_____	_____	_____	_____
_____	_____	_____	_____	_____
_____	_____	_____	_____	_____

Check your answers. Practice saying the phrases with your partner.
Or repeat the phrases after your teacher or the speaker on the audio.

6, 12

Supplement 14. Selecting Vowel Sounds to Study

Problems with vowel sounds depend on the individual and her or his first language. The activities below will help you choose the sounds *you* need to practice.

Exercise 1 If a sound is not in your first language, it might be hard to hear. Listen to each set of phrases. Is it easy or hard to hear a difference? If hard, go to the supplement for more practice.

Example	/ɛ/	**te**st it				
	/eʸ/	**ta**ste it	☐ Easy	☐ Hard	☞	*Supplement 16*
1.	/ɪ/	don't **hi**t it				
	/iʸ/	don't **hea**t it	☐ Easy	☐ Hard	☞	*Supplement 15*
2.	/ɛ/	a bad **pen**				
	/eʸ/	a bad **pain**	☐ Easy	☐ Hard	☞	*Supplement 16*
3.	/æ/	**Dan** Smith				
	/ɑ/	**Don** Smith	☐ Easy	☐ Hard	☞	*Supplement 18*
4.	/ʌ/	my **luck**				
	/ɑ/	my **lock**	☐ Easy	☐ Hard	☞	*Supplement 18*
5.	/ʌ/	your **cup**				
	/æ/	your **cap**	☐ Easy	☐ Hard	☞	*Supplement 18*
6.	/ʊ/	**pull** it				
	/uʷ/	**pool** it	☐ Easy	☐ Hard	☞	*Supplement 17*

Exercise 2 Look at the Pronunciation Checklist in Chapter 1. Did your teacher note vowel sounds that were difficult for you to say? What were they?

_____

_____

Vowel Practices

Supplement 15.

/iʸ/   heat   –   /ɪ/   hit

Listening Activity 1 Listen to the /iʸ/ and /ɪ/ sounds.

/iʸ/.../ɪ/.../iʸ/.../ɪ/.../iʸ/.../ɪ/.../iʸ/.../ɪ/

Listening Activity 2 Listen to the word pairs below.

Vowel 1. /iʸ/—Vowel 2. /ɪ/

eat–it	leap–lip	heater–hitter
seen–sin	steal–still	leave–live
heat–hit	feet–fit	feel–fill

You will hear two words from the list above. If the words are the same (*eat–eat*), write __S__. If the words are different (*eat–it*), write __D__.

1. _____   4. _____   7. _____

2. _____   5. _____   8. _____

3. _____   6. _____   9. _____

🔑 Check your answers.

Listen again. Now listen to both words in each pair. Repeat the activity until you are confident of your answers.

Listening Activity 3 Listen to the teacher or the speaker on the audio say the prompt. Circle the correct answer.

Prompt
1. ___ Can you **feel** it?
   ___ Can you **fill** it?

Answer
a. ___ It's cold.
b. ___ It's empty.

2. ___ He wants to **leave** there.
   ___ He wants to **live** there.

a. ___ He doesn't like it.
b. ___ He likes it.

3. ___ They need better **hea**ters.
   ___ They need better **hit**ters.

a. ___ They're cold.
b. ___ They're losing the game.

4. ___ Where's the sh**ee**p?
   ___ Where's the sh**i**p?

a. ___ In the meadow.
b. ___ In the harbor.

🔑 Check your answers.

Listen again. Now listen to both prompts and answers.

195

Listening Activity 4 Listen to the paragraph. Fill in the blanks with words that have /iʸ/ and /ɪ/.

Counting Sheep

1 Many _____ have trouble falling _____. Some try counting _____.

2 They try to imagine the same _____ happening over and over, like sheep _____

3 one after the other. By _____ of one thing, they forget other _____. They

4 may actually go to _____ because they are bored!

🔑 Check your answers.

▲ **Figure 32** /iʸ/

The front part of the tongue is pushed close to the roof of the mouth. During the sound, the front of the tongue moves a little higher. The lips are spread. The lips and tongue are tense.
Common Spellings:
-ee-, -ea-: seen, meat
-e-e: these, Steve
-e: me, he

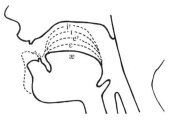

▲ **Figure 33 Front Vowels**

▲ **Figure 34** /ɪ/

The front part of the tongue is not as high as it is for /iʸ/. The lips and tongue are relaxed.
Common Spelling:
-i-:   big, win

Exercise 1 Look at Figure 33. Repeat the front vowels:

   /iʸ/ . . . /ɪ/ . . . /eʸ/ . . . /ɛ/ . . . /æ/

Now repeat the highest front vowels 1 and 2:

   /iʸ/ . . . /ɪ/ . . . /iʸ/ . . . /ɪ/ . . . /iʸ/ . . . /ɪ/ . . . /iʸ/ . . . /ɪ/

Exercise 2 Repeat the word pairs in Listening Activity 2.

Exercise 3 Repeat each prompt and answer in Listening Activity 3. Or, work with a partner.

> *Student A*: Check a prompt and say it to *Student B*.
> *Student B*: Check the answer and say it to *Student A*.

Exercise 4 Practice these words with /iʸ/ and /ɪ/. These are key words in the dialogue below.

> Vowel 1. /iʸ/: leave, eat, cheese, seen, cheap
> Vowel 2. /ɪ/: Mick's, terRIfic, conVINCED

Listen to the dialogue several times. Then say it several times *with* the speakers. Or practice the dialogue with a partner.

> *Lunchtime*

A: Are you ready to **LEAVE**?

B: Yeah, let's **EAT**.

A: How about **MICK'S?** They have the best mac and **CHEESE**.

B: I've never **EAT**en there. I've never even **SEEN** it!

A: Well, the food's ter**RI**fic, and it's **CHEAP**.

B: Okay! You've con**VINCED** me.

Exercise 5 Find *Counting Sheep* in Listening Activity 4 in the Answer Key. Read it chorally with your class or with the speakers until you can read it fluently.

Now record it. Listen to your pronunciation of the underlined words with /iʸ/ and /ɪ/. Repeat until you are satisfied with your recording.

Communicative Practice . . . planning a meal

You and your roommate are inviting friends for dinner. Each of you has menu ideas below. Decide who will be *Student A* and who will be *Student B*. Add your own suggestions.

Words with /iʸ/ and /ɪ/ are boldfaced. If the word has Vowel 1—/iʸ/, write 1 above it. If the word has Vowel 2—/ɪ/, write 2 above it. Practice saying the words.

Discuss what food to prepare.

Student A:

Appetizer	Entrée	Vegetable	Salad	Dessert
1 **bean dip** and **chips**	**beef**	**spin**ach	**Greek** salad	**cheese**cake
_____	_____	_____	_____	_____

Student B:

Appetizer	Entrée	Vegetable	Salad	Dessert
cheese and crackers	**shrimp**	**green beans**	**field greens**	ice **cream**
_____	_____	_____	_____	_____

Tell the rest of the class what you are having. Which pair is fixing the best meal?

Supplement 16.

/e^y/ late – /ɛ/ let

Listening Activity 1 Listen to the /e^y/ and /ɛ/ sounds. (6, 25)

/e^y/. . ./ɛ/. . ./e^y/. . ./ɛ/. . ./e^y/. . ./ɛ/. . ./e^y/. . ./ɛ/

Listening Activity 2 Listen to the word pairs. (6, 26)

Vowel 3. /e^y/—Vowel 4. /ɛ/		
wait–wet	pain–pen	date–debt
taste–test	late–let	whale–well
main–men	paper–pepper	age–edge

You will hear two words from the list above. If the words are the same (*wait–wait*), write _S_. If the words are different (*wait–wet*), write _D_.

1. ______ **4.** ______ **7.** ______

2. ______ **5.** ______ **8.** ______

3. ______ **6.** ______ **9.** ______

Check your answers.

Listen again. Now listen to both words in each pair. Repeat the activity until you are confident of your answers. (6, 27)

Listening Activity 3 Listen to the teacher or the speaker on the audio say the prompt. Circle the correct answer. (6, 28)

Prompt	*Answer*
1. ___ Do you have a big date? ___ Do you have a big debt?	a. ___ Yes, we're going to a nice restaurant. b. ___ No, I paid it off.
2. ___ I have a terrible pain. ___ I have a terrible pen.	a. ___ Maybe you should call your doctor. b. ___ You can borrow mine.
3. ___ Was that your first taste? ___ Was that your first test?	a. ___ Yes. It was delicious. b. ___ Yes. It was easy.
4. ___ Where's the paper? ___ Where's the pepper?	a. ___ Aisle 2, with office supplies. b. ___ Aisle 5 with spices.

Check your answers.

Listening Activity 4 Listen to these facts. Fill in the blanks with words that have /eʸ/ and /ɛ/.

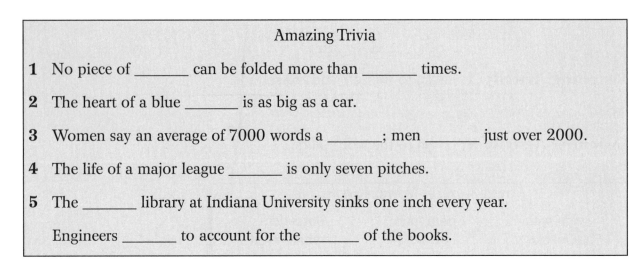

Amazing Trivia

1 No piece of _____ can be folded more than _____ times.

2 The heart of a blue _____ is as big as a car.

3 Women say an average of 7000 words a _____; men _____ just over 2000.

4 The life of a major league _____ is only seven pitches.

5 The _____ library at Indiana University sinks one inch every year.

Engineers _____ to account for the _____ of the books.

Check your answers.

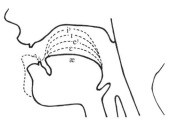

▲ **Figure 35 Front Vowels**

/eʸ/ Once you begin the sound, the front of the tongue and jaw move higher. The lips are spread. The tongue and jaw are tense.
Common Spellings:
-a-e: late, shape
-ai-:   rain, mail
-ay: day, gray

/ɛ/ The tongue is lower and the mouth is more open than for /eʸ/. The tongue and jaw are relaxed. The tongue is motionless.
Common Spelling:
-e-:   pen, tent

Exercise 1 Look at Figure 35. Repeat the front vowels:

/iʸ/. . .   /ɪ/. . .   /eʸ/. . .   /ɛ/. . .   /æ/

Now repeat vowels 3 and 4:

/eʸ/. . .   /ɛ/. . .   /eʸ/. . .   /ɛ/. . .   /eʸ/. . .   /ɛ/. . .   /eʸ/. . .   /ɛ/

Exercise 2 Repeat the word pairs in Listening Activity 2.

Exercise 3 Repeat each prompt and answer in Listening Activity 3. Or, work with a partner.

> *Student A*: Check a prompt and say it to *Student B*.
> *Student B*: Check the answer and say it to *Student A*.

Exercise 4 Practice these words with /eʸ/ and /ɛ/. They are key words in the dialogue.

> Vowel 3. /eʸ/: great, day, shape, TRAINer, exPLAINS
> Vowel 4. /ɛ/: Jen

Listen to the dialogue several times and then say it several times *with* the speakers. Or practice the dialogue with a partner.

> *High School Reunion*

A: Wow! Check out **JEN**.

B: She looks **GREAT**! She hasn't aged a **DAY**.

A: How does she stay in such great **SHAPE**?

B: She must work out every **DAY**.

A: Look! It says she's a personal **TRAIN**er.

B: Well, **THAT** exPLAINS it.

Exercise 5 Find *Amazing Trivia* in Listening Activity 4 in the Answer Key. Read it chorally with your class or with the speakers until you can read it fluently.

Now record it. Listen to your pronunciation of the underlined words with /eʸ/ and /ɛ/. Repeat until you are satisfied with your recording.

Communicative Practice . . . twenty-four-hour day

How do you use your time? See the sample schedule below.
Words and stressed syllables with /eʸ/ and /ɛ/ are in bold type. If the words have vowel 3, /eʸ/ as in *late,* write 3 above them. If they have Vowel 4, /ɛ/ as in *let,* write 4 above them.

Then create your schedule for a typical weekday. Your time should add up to 24 hours.

Sample Schedule: <u>Wednesday</u>	
Sleep	7 ½ hours
³ **Bathe, dress**	½ hour
Make and eat **break**fast	½ hour
Read the **paper**	½ hour
Get to school	½ hour
Attend classes	7 hours
Go home	½ hour
Do homework	2 hours
Do e-**mail**	1 hour
Make and eat dinner	½ hour
Watch **tel**evision	1 hour
Take a walk	½ hour
Make phone calls	1 hours
Get ready for **bed**/read	<u>1 hour</u>
Total time **spent** =	24 hours

Your schedule: _____

_____

_____

_____

_____

_____

_____

_____

_____

_____

_____

_____

_____

_____

With your partner or small group, talk about your schedule.

What do you **spend** the most time doing?

What would you like to **spend** more time doing?

What would you like to **spend** less time doing?

Supplement 17.

/u^w/ too   –   /ʊ/ took

Listening Activity 1 Listen to the /u^w/ and /ʊ/ sounds.

/u^w/. . ./ʊ/. . ./u^w/. . ./ʊ/. . ./u^w/. . ./ʊ/. . ./u^w/. . ./ʊ/

Listening Activity 2 Listen to the word pairs.

Vowel 9. /u^w/—Vowel 10. /ʊ/

fool–full	suit–soot
pool–pull	who'd–hood
Luke–look	stewed–stood

You will hear two words from the list above. If the words are the same (*fool–fool*), write _S_. If the words are different (*fool–full*), write _D_.

1. ____   4. ____

2. ____   5. ____

3. ____   6. ____

 Check your answers.

Listen again. Now listen to both words in each pair. Repeat the activity until you are confident of your answers.

Listening Activity 3 Dictation. Listen to the teacher or the speaker on the audio read the words. Write them in the correct column below.

/u^w/—too	/ʊ/—took
shoe	

Check your answers.

Listen again.

Listening Activity 4 Listen to the paragraph. Fill in the blanks with words that have /uʷ/ and /ʊ/.

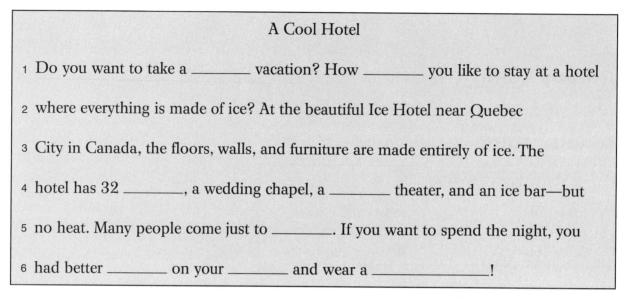

A Cool Hotel

1 Do you want to take a _____ vacation? How _____ you like to stay at a hotel

2 where everything is made of ice? At the beautiful Ice Hotel near Quebec

3 City in Canada, the floors, walls, and furniture are made entirely of ice. The

4 hotel has 32 _____, a wedding chapel, a _____ theater, and an ice bar—but

5 no heat. Many people come just to _____. If you want to spend the night, you

6 had better _____ on your _____ and wear a _____!

🔑 Check your answers.

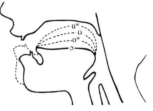

▲ **Figure 36** /uʷ/
During the sound, the back of the tongue moves higher and the lip rounding increases slightly. The lips and tongue are tense.
Common Spellings:
-oo-:   room, food
-u-e, -ue: June, blue

▲ **Figure 37** Back Vowels

▲ **Figure 38** /ʊ/
/ʊ/— The tongue is lower than for /uʷ/. The lips are slightly rounded. The lips and tongue are relaxed. The tongue is motionless.
Common Spelling:
-oo-:   look, cook
-u-:   full, put
Common Words:
-ou-:   could, should, would

Exercise 1 Look at Figure 37. Repeat the back vowels:

/uʷ/. . ./ʊ/. . ./oʷ/. . ./ɔ/

Now repeat the highest back vowels 9 and 10:

/uʷ/. . ./ʊ/. . ./uʷ/. . ./ʊ/. . ./uʷ/. . ./ʊ/. . ./uʷ/. . ./ʊ/

Exercise 2 Repeat the word pairs in Listening Activity 2.

Exercise 3 Repeat the list of words with /uʷ/and /ʊ/ in Listening Activity 3.

Exercise 4 Practice these words with /uʷ/ and /ʊ/.
They are key words in the dialogue.

    Vowel 3. /uʷ/: noon, two, news, school, do, exCUSE, truth

    Vowel 4. /ʊ/: good

Listen to the dialogue several times. Then say the dialogue several times *with* the speakers. Or, practice the dialogue with a partner.

            Early Riser

A: Oh, **GOOD**! I woke up **EAR**ly.

B: It's **NOT** early. It's **NOON**!

A: But my clock says eight-twenty-**TWO**.

B: I hate to break the bad **NEWS**, but it's after**NOON**.

A: I was supposed to be at **SCHOOL** by noon. What should I **DO**?

    Help me think of a good ex**CUSE**.

B: Why don't you just tell the **TRUTH**?

Exercise 5 Find *A Cool Hotel* in Listening Activity 4 in the Answer Key. Read it chorally with your class or with the speakers until you can read it fluently.

Now record it. Listen to your pronunciation of the underlined words with /uʷ/ and /ʊ/. Repeat until you are satisfied with your recording.

Communicative Practice . . . I would/wouldn't do that!

Do you like adventures? Do you like to take risks?

Look at the key phrases and activities in the box below. The words with Vowel 9—/uʷ/ as in *too* and Vowel 10—/ʊ/ as in *took* are in bold type. Write 9 or 10 over the bold words and practice saying them.

Discuss which things you would and would not do. Talk about why.

I **would** . . .

I **would**n't . . .

I **could do** that.

I **could**n't **do** that.

Would you . . .

Why **would**n't **you** . . .

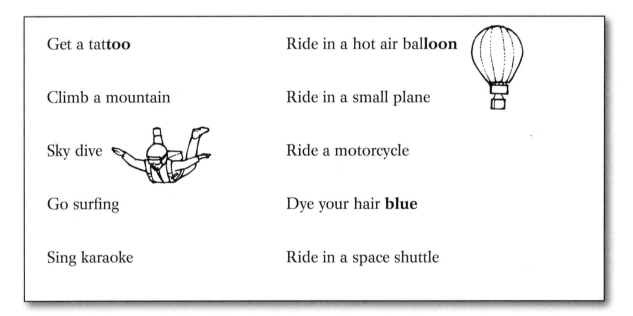

Get a tat**too**	Ride in a hot air bal**loon**
Climb a mountain	Ride in a small plane
Sky dive	Ride a motorcycle
Go surfing	Dye your hair **blue**
Sing karaoke	Ride in a space shuttle

Supplement 18.

/æ/ cap	–	/ʌ/ cup	–	/ɑ/ cop

Listening Activity 1 Vowels 5 /æ/ and 7 /ʌ/ do not exist in many languages. Listen carefully. *(6, 46)*

/æ/. . ./ʌ/. . ./ɑ/   /æ/. . ./ʌ/. . ./ɑ/   /æ/. . ./ʌ/. . ./ɑ/

Listening Activity 2 Listen to the word pairs. *(6, 47)*

Vowel 5. /æ/ – Vowel 7. /ʌ/	Vowel 5. /æ/ – Vowel 8. /ɑ/	Vowel 7. /ʌ/ – Vowel 8. /ɑ/
cap–cup	cap–cop	cup–cop
hat–hut	hat–hot	hut–hot
bag–bug	add–odd	nut–not
mad–mud	Ann–on	luck–lock

You will hear two words from the pairs above. If the words are the same (*cap–cap*), write _S_. If the words are different (*cap–cup*), write _D_.

1. _____   5. _____   9. _____

2. _____   6. _____   10. _____

3. _____   7. _____   11. _____

4. _____   8. _____   12. _____

🔑 Check your answers.

Listen again. Now listen to both words in each pair. Repeat the activity until you are confident of your answers. *(6, 48)*

Listening Activity 3 Listen to the words. Write them in the correct column. *(6, 49)*

/æ/ cap	/ʌ/ cup	/ɑ/ cop
fact		

Listening Activity 4 Listen to the paragraph. Fill in the blanks with words that have /æ/, /ʌ/, and /ɑ/.

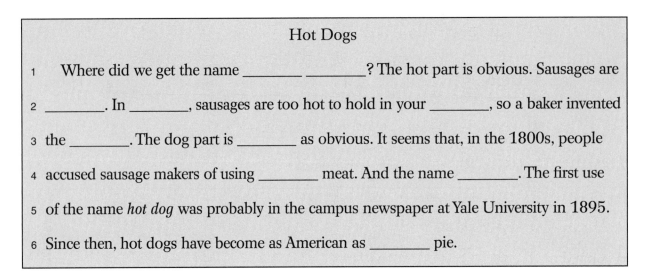

Hot Dogs

1   Where did we get the name _____ _____? The hot part is obvious. Sausages are

2   _____. In _____, sausages are too hot to hold in your _____, so a baker invented

3   the _____. The dog part is _____ as obvious. It seems that, in the 1800s, people

4   accused sausage makers of using _____ meat. And the name _____. The first use

5   of the name *hot dog* was probably in the campus newspaper at Yale University in 1895.

6   Since then, hot dogs have become as American as _____ pie.

Check your answers.

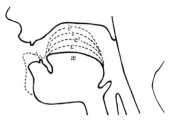

▲ **Figure 39:** Front Vowels

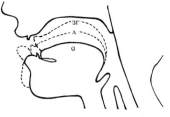

▲ **Figure 40:** Central Vowels

▲ **Figure 41:** /æ/

The mouth is open wide. The tongue is low and forward. Lips are slightly spread.
Common Spelling:
-a- : sad, bank

▲ **Figure 42:** /ʌ/

The mouth is open a little. The jaw, tongue, and lips are relaxed and neutral.
Common Spelling:
-u-: bus, much
Common Words:
-o-: month, love, won, some mother

▲ **Figure 43:** /ɑ/

The mouth drops open a lot. Make this sound if the doctor wants to see into your throat.
Common Spelling:
-o-: hot, stop
*In some accents in the United States and Canada, there is little difference between /ɔ/ caught and /ɑ/ cot.

Exercise 1 Look at Figure 39. Repeat the front vowels:

/iʸ/... /ɪ/... /eʸ/... /ɛ/... /æ/

Look at Figure 40. Repeat the central vowels.

/ɜr/.../ʌ/.../ɑ/

Now repeat the lowest front vowel 5 and the central vowels 7 and 8.

/æ/.../ʌ/.../ɑ/   /æ/.../ʌ/.../ɑ/   /æ/.../ʌ/.../ɑ/

Exercise 2 Repeat the word pairs in Listening Activity 2.

Exercise 3 Repeat the list of words with /æ/, /ʌ/, and /ɑ/ in Listening Activity 3.

Exercise 4 Practice these words with /æ/, /ʌ/, and /ɑ/. They are key words in the dialogue.

Vowel 5. /æ/: that, thanks, hat, CANcer
Vowel 7. /ʌ/: lunch, bus, fun, MONey
Vowel 8. /ɑ/: hot

Listen to the dialogue several times. Then say the dialogue several times *with* the speakers. Or, practice the dialogue with a partner.

Fun Run

A: Aren't you going to eat **LUNCH?**

B: Not to**DAY**. I've got to catch the **BUS**. I'm doing a **FUN** run.

A: . . . but running isn't **FUN**.

B: Well, it's for a good **CAUSE**. We're raising funds for **CAN**cer research.

A: Oh, **THAT'S** nice. Here's some **MON**ey.

B: **THANKS!**

A: Oh, and wear this **HAT**! The sun's going to be **HOT** today.

Exercise 5 Find *Hot Dogs* in Listening Activity 4 in the Answer Key. Read it chorally with your class or with the speakers until you can read it fluently.

Now record it. Listen to your pronunciation of the underlined words with /æ/, /ʌ/, and /ɑ/. Repeat until you are satisfied with your recording.

Communicative Practice . . . odd laws

Here are some strange laws. Many are old. Most are not enforced. But they still exist.

Look at the vowel sounds in bold type. Write Vowel 5—/æ/, Vowel 7— /ʌ/, or Vowel 8 — /ɑ/ above each bold vowel. Practice saying the words.

It is illegal . . .

To Do What?	*Where?*
To sell c**a**bbage on S**u**nday	New Jersey
For d**o**gs and c**a**ts to fight	North Carolina
To fish in your paj**a**mas	Chicago, Illinois
To r**u**n out of g**a**s	Youngstown, Ohio
To put c**a**ttle on a school b**u**s	Florida
To charge a bald m**a**n more than 25 cents for a haircut	Louisiana
To blow your nose in p**u**blic	Maine
To wear a h**a**t while d**a**ncing	Fargo, North Dakota
To set a mouse tr**a**p without a h**u**nting license	California
Finally, a person must take a b**a**th once a year	Kentucky

Then, discuss these questions with your partner or small group.

Which two laws do you think are the oddest of all?

Why do you think some of these laws were made?

Information Gap Activities

Chapter 4: Final Consonant Sounds and Linking

Exercise 4 *Student A:* Speaker

1. Meet me at home at nine.

2. You have food in your teeth.

3. Did you do your homework?

4. What time do you want to leave?

Chapter 10: Basic Rhythm: Reduced Words

Get Set!

Student A:

A: The party'll be on Sunday in the Terrace Apartments.

   Pause

A: That's right . . . 427.

   Pause

A: I can take you.

   Pause

A: I can't pick you up before noon.

   Pause

A: We're having salad and sandwiches.

   Pause

A: I'll ask for volunteers to help clean up.

   Pause

A: Victor can't come, but he can get the gift.

   Pause

A: Don't worry. Sam'll love it. Snakes are quiet. And you only have to feed them once a month!

Supplement 7

Student B: Planner

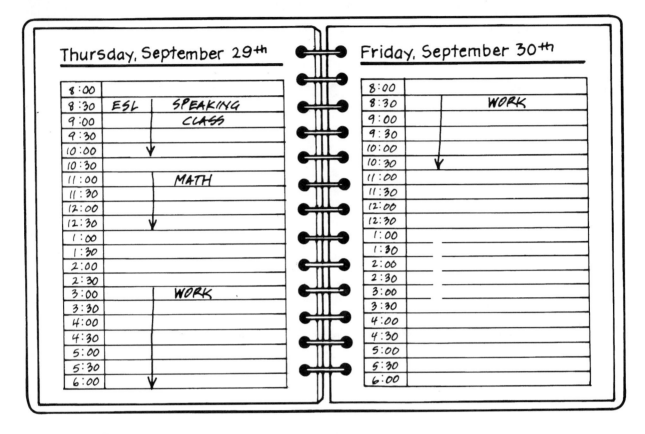

Thursday, September 29th		
8:00		
8:30	ESL	SPEAKING
9:00		CLASS
9:30		
10:00	↓	
10:30		
11:00		MATH
11:30		
12:00		
12:30	↓	
1:00		
1:30		
2:00		
2:30		
3:00		WORK
3:30		
4:00		
4:30		
5:00		
5:30		
6:00	↓	

Friday, September 30th		
8:00		
8:30		WORK
9:00		
9:30		
10:00		
10:30	↓	
11:00		
11:30		
12:00		
12:30		
1:00		
1:30		
2:00		
2:30		
3:00		
3:30		
4:00		
4:30		
5:00		
5:30		
6:00		

Appendix 1: Personal Key Word List

Word	Syllables	Stress	Typical Phrase/Sentence
1.			
2.			
3.			
4.			
5.			
6.			
7.			
8.			
9.			
10.			
11.			
12.			
13.			
14.			
15.			
16.			
17.			
18.			
19.			
20.			

Appendix 2: Common Words with Omitted Syllables

Native speakers usually omit one of the syllables in these words. They omit the unstressed syllable that comes after the syllable with primary stress.

1. EV e̶ ning
   - every evening
   - Saturday evening
   - Good evening!

2. CHOC o̶ late
   - chocolate cake
   - chocolate sauce
   - chocolate milk

3. CAM e̶ ra
   - video camera
   - security camera
   - digital camera

4. BUS i̶ ness
   - small business
   - family business
   - business associate

5. VEG e̶ ta ble
   - bowl of vegetable soup
   - fresh vegetables
   - green vegetables

6. INT e̶ res ting
   - It's interesting.
   - very interesting
   - quite interesting

7. DIFF e̶ rent
   - different from
   - completely different
   - different ways

8. FAV o̶ rite
   - favorite one
   - favorite book
   - favorite teacher

9. REST u̶a̶ rant
   - local restaurant
   - popular restaurant
   - Chinese restaurant

10. FAM i̶ ly
    - the whole family
    - family friends
    - family income

Appendix 3: Suffixes and Word Stress

These are the more common suffixes with simple relationships to word stress. You will find exceptions.

1. **Stress the syllable immediately before these suffixes:**

   a. -i suffixes

-ial	MEmory	→	meMOr**ial**
-ian	LIbrary	→	liBRAr**ian**
-ic	ARtist	→	arTISt**ic**
-ical	psyCHOlogy	→	psychoLOg**ical**
-ify	HUmid	→	huMId**ify**
-ion (-sion and -tion)	DEmonstrate	→	demonSTRAt**ion**
-ious	MYStery	→	mysTER**ious**
-ity	POSsible	→	possiBIl**ity**

b.	-cracy	DEmocrat	→	deMO**cracy**
c.	-graphy	PHOtograph	→	phoTO**graphy**
d.	-logy	ZOO	→	zoOl**ogy**
e.	-eous	COUrage	→	couRAg**eous**

   Note these exceptions: aRITHmetic, ARabic, POlitics, TElevision

2. Stress these suffixes when they end words:

a.	-ee	trainEE		d.	-ette	dinETTE
b.	-ain (verbs)	mainTAIN		e.	-esque	picturESQUE
c.	-ese	ChinESE		f.	-ique	techNIQUE

Note these exceptions: COFfee, comMITtee

Note: **The stress does not change when these suffixes are added.**

a.	-able	COMfort	→	COMfortable
b.	-age	perCENT	→	perCENTage
c.	-ful	PLENty	→	PLENtiful
d.	-hood	NEIGHbor	→	NEIGHborhood
e.	-less	PENny	→	PENniless
f.	-ly	CAREful	→	CAREfully
g.	-ment	GOVern	→	GOVernment
h.	-ness	HAPpy	→	HAPpiness
i.	-or/er	MANage	→	MANager

Appendix 4: Feedback Form for Chapter 13— Extend Your Skills . . . Giving Instructions

PRONUNCIATION FEATURE: Thought Groups and Pausing

Speaker: _____   Date: _____

Listener: _____

1. The topic was clearly stated.   _____ Yes   _____ No

   What was the topic? _____

2. I could follow the steps.   _____ Yes   _____ No _____ Somewhat

   How many steps did the process have? _____

3. The speaker was easiest to understand when he/she . . .

   _____

4. The speaker was hardest to understand when he/she . . .

   _____

5. Maybe the speaker could . . .

   _____

Answer Key for *Prime-Time Practices*

Chapter 5
Answers are underlined. All words ending in *-s* are highlighted.

ODD JOBS

Do you work to live or live to work? The answer probably depends on your job. These five people love their jobs. Do any of these jobs appeal to you?

- Cindy works in a potato chip factory. If she sees chips that are overcooked, she removes them—or eats them!
- Louis is a page turner. He turns pages of music for pianists when they play in New York City.
- Brian tests video games. He plays games eight hours a day five days a week, and he never gets bored.
- Jeff dives for golf balls in lakes in Florida. Every week he finds about 25,000 balls and sells them for five to ten cents each.
- John is a taste tester. He eats ice cream four to five hours a day and gets paid to do it!

Chapter 6

Campus Slang and Idioms

Step 1: Match the underlined word/phrase with the definition.

1. _b_ Ari doesn't drink. He offered to be our <u>designated driver</u>.
2. _d_ I <u>flunked</u> my math midterm.
3. _a_ I <u>aced</u> my biology final.
4. _e_ My parents <u>freaked out</u> when they heard about my car wreck.
5. _f_ I wasn't hurt, but my car was <u>totaled</u>.
6. _c_ Maria is totally <u>psyched</u> about her ski trip.

Step 2: Decide how to pronounce the *-ed* words.

1. /ˈdɛzɪgneʸtəd/   4. /friʸkt/
2. /flʌŋkt/   5. /toʷtld/
3. /eʸst/   6. /saɪkt/

Chapter 7

a. spent time with friends	<u>hung OUT</u>
b. pay	<u>SHELL out*</u>
c. ate a lot of food at one time	<u>pigged OUT</u>
d. something that costs more than it is worth	<u>RIPoff</u>
e. to complete late or missed work	<u>catch UP</u>

*Usually speakers say "shell OUT." In this case, however, "shell out" has a direct object noun (cash), and most speakers would say "SHELL out CASH."

Answer Key for Consonant Supplements

Supplement 1. Phonetic Alphabet

Exercise 1

1. /k/ Canada
2. /t/ Thailand
3. /tʃ/ China
4. /y/ United States
5. /g/ Greece

Exercise 2

1. /t/ Thomas, Tyler
2. /s/ Sara, Samantha
3. /dʒ/ Jessica, Joshua
4. /k/ Kyle, Christopher
5. /m/ Michael, Megan

Supplement 2. Consonant Overview

Exercise 2

	Continuant	Stop
Examples:	____ less	✓ let
	✓ bus	____ but
1.	✓ boss	____ bought
2.	✓ bath	____ bat
3.	____ both	✓ boat
4.	____ a nice manager	✓ a night manager
5.	____ the rice cereal	✓ the right cereal
6.	✓ he's gone	____ he'd gone
7.	____ lost his prize	✓ lost his pride
8.	✓ which size	____ which side
9.	____ he plays piano	✓ he played piano
10.	____ place setting	✓ plate setting

Exercise 3

1. /p/ Park — (both lips) — lips–teeth — tongue–teeth
2. /f/ First — both lips — (lips–teeth) — tongue–teeth
3. /w/ Washington — (both lips) — lips–teeth — tongue–teeth
4. /θ/ Fourth — both lips — lips–teeth — (tongue–teeth)
5. /l/ Lake — (tongue–gum ridge) — tongue–hard palate — tongue–soft palate
6. /n/ Pine — (tongue–gum ridge) — tongue–hard palate — tongue–soft palate
7. /k/ Oak — tongue–gum ridge — tongue–hard palate — (tongue–soft palate)

Supplement 4. Initial /p/ – /b/   /t/ – /d/   /k/ – /g/

Listening Activity 1

1. pack–back (D)

2. peach–peach (S)

3. appear–a beer (D)

4. dime–dime (S)

5. tie–die (D)

6. tore–door (D)

7. come–gum (D)

8. could–could (S)

9. curl–girl (D)

Listening Activity 2

1. b. Yes, and we had it for dinner.

2. a. It's a vitamin.

3. a. More than 20 percent?

4. b. No, silver.

Listening Activity 3

Tying the Knot: Who Pays?
1   The cost of an average wedding in 2005 was almost <u>twenty</u>-three thousand
2   dollars.* Who <u>pays</u> the bill? Traditionally, the bride's <u>parents</u> cover most of
3   the costs. They pay for the ceremony and the reception. The groom's parent's
4   <u>pick</u> up the cost of the rehearsal dinner. As <u>costs</u> climb, however, <u>customs</u>
5   are changing. Today 60 <u>percent</u> of couples pay some of their wedding costs.
6   It is also becoming more <u>common</u> for the bride's parents, the groom's
7   parents, and the <u>couple</u> to divide costs equally.

Supplement 5. Final /p/ – /b/   /t/ – /d/   /k/ – /g/

Listening Activity 1

1. lap–lab (D)

2. cap–cab (D)

3. robe–robe (S)

4. state–state (S)

5. debt–dead (D)

6. feet–feed (D)

7. back–bag (D)

8. dock–dock (S)

9. lock–log (D)

Listening Activity 2

/p/ or /b/

1. Did you have any trouble finding a ca<u>b</u>?

2. We're going to look for a pu<u>b</u>. Do you want to come?

3. You didn't lose your notebook. It's in your la<u>p</u>.

/t/ or /d/

4. She made the be<u>t</u>.

5. I've lost the bea<u>t</u>.

6. Louis fell off his bike and hurt his arm. I don't know if he can <u>ride</u>.

/k/ or /g/

7. Just put the coats in the ba<u>g</u>.

8. That's not my pi<u>ck</u>.

9. We need to go to the hardware store for a lo<u>g</u>.

Listening Activity 3

Tele-work Jobs
1   More and more employees want to tele-work from home. Some
2   people don't want to drive or <u>ride</u> a bus to and from work. Other people say it's
3   <u>hard</u> to balance a <u>job</u> with their lives. They <u>need</u> more time at home to care
4   for a parent or a sick child. Employers think tele-work is a <u>good</u> idea too.
5
6   They don't have to <u>provide</u> office space, so they save on rent. They don't have to
7   train new staff because there's less <u>job</u> turnover. And would you believe that
most employees do more work when they are at home?

Supplement 6. /m/ - /n/ - /ŋ/

Listening Activity 2

1. some–some (S)	**4.** done–done (S)	**7.** sun–sung (D)
2. comb–cone (D)	**5.** same–sane (D)	**8.** thin–thing (D)
3. warm–warn (D)	**6.** gain–gain (S)	**9.** wing–wing (S)

Listening Activity 3

Response

1. b. Yes. With a scoop of vanilla.	**3.** a. Hi Tim! Nice to meet you.
2. b. To tie up the boat.	**4.** b. Yes. He has no time to prepare.

Listening Activity 4

Nine Lives
1   <u>Some</u> people say cats have <u>nine</u> lives. That is because cats usually survive
2   <u>long</u> falls. After they fall, they <u>seem</u> to return to life. Why? They land
3   <u>on</u> all four paws, and they bend their legs <u>when</u> they land. A study in
4   New York showed cats were more likely to survive when they fell
5   from <u>seven</u> to 32 floors than when they fell <u>from</u> two to six floors. That is
6
7   because the cats had <u>time</u> to spread their legs into an umbrella shape
to slow <u>down</u> their fall.

Supplement 7. /θ/

Listening Activity 2

1. think–sink (D)	**5.** tank–tank (S)	**9.** bath–bat (D)
2. sing–sing (S)	**6.** three–three (S)	**10.** both–both (S)
3. fourth–fourth (S)	**7.** through–true (D)	**11.** math–mat (D)
4. mouth–mouse (D)	**8.** thin–tin (D)	**12.** tenth–tent (D)

Listening Activity 3

1. b. No. He's out-of-shape.
2. a. We can do homework.
3. a. He can't keep a secret.
4. b. It's finished.

Listening Activity 4

Earth Day
1   Each year we celebrate <u>Earth</u> Day, and <u>thousands </u>of school children in Canada and the
2   United States do what they can to protect and improve the environment. One
3   year students in Winnipeg started bringing trash-free lunches to school every day. Now they
4   <u>throw</u> nothing away. <u>Fourth</u> grade students in Texas raised more than one <u>thousand</u> dollars at a
5   garage sale. They used the money to protect twenty-
6   <u>three</u> acres of rainforest in Costa Rica. And students in Pennsylvania made
7   <u>cloth</u> grocery bags for their parents to use year after year.

Supplement 8. /ʃ/ - /tʃ/ - /dʒ/

Listening Activity 2

1. see–she (D)
2. sue–shoe (D)
3. show–show (S)
4. seat–sheet (D)
5. chip–chip (S)
6. too–chew (D)
7. beat–beach (D)
8. Pete–Pete (S)
9. she's–cheese (D)
10. cheat–cheat (S)
11. wish–wish (S)
12. wash–watch (D)
13. gin–gin (S)
14. chose–Joe's (D)
15. choke–choke (S)
16. rich–ridge (D)

Listening Activity 3

1. a. Yes, in the third row.
2. a. My car.
3. a. Yes. It's good for dancing.
4. a. Is it already the end of February?
5. a. But nobody laughed.

Listening Activity 4

Short Vacations
1   Do you live to work or work to live? Many workers in the United States are asking
2   themselves that <u>question</u>. Why? They get <u>shorter</u> vacations than workers in most
3   other industrialized <u>nations</u>. The average worker in the United States takes ten
4   <u>vacation</u> days a year after three years on the <u>job</u>. U.S. law does not guarantee
5   workers any vacation time. <u>Chinese</u> workers are guaranteed 15 vacation days.
6   Workers in <u>Japan</u> are guaranteed ten days and take an <u>average</u> of 18. <u>Danish</u>
7   and <u>French</u> workers are guaranteed 25 paid vacation days and take an average of 30.

/ʃ/	**sh**orter	**n**ations	va**c**ation
/tʃ/	ques**t**ion	**Ch**inese	Fren**ch**
/dʒ/	**j**ob	**J**apan	avera**ge**

Supplement 9. /l/ – /r/

Listening Activity 2

1. right–right (S) **4.** lock–rock (D) **7.** collect–correct (D)

2. long–long (S) **5.** long–long (S) **8.** pilot–pirate (D)

3. lead–read (D) **6.** lap–rap (D) **9.** tire–tire (S)

Listening Activity 3

1. b. No. It's right.

2. a. No. It's still dark.

3. a.

4. b. For the doors.

Listening Activity 4

Being a Lefty
1   One in every ten people is <u>left</u>-handed. But did you know that most
2   left-handed people are also left ear, left eye, and left-footed as well? A
3   left-handed person uses his left eye to <u>look</u> through a microscope. He <u>leads</u>
4   with his <u>left</u> foot when walking. He winks more <u>easily</u> with his left eye. And
5   his <u>smile</u> curves up more on the left side. The <u>reverse</u> is true for <u>right</u>-handed
6   people.

Supplement 10. Initial Consonant Clusters

Listening Activity 1

(pace) place   (box) blocks   state (estate)

say (stay)   (fee) free   train (to rain)

back (black)   sell (smell)   (slow) so low

Exercise 1 Note: Less common words are in parentheses. Speakers on audio will not include those words in the practice.

1. brake

2. play, pray

3. glass, grass

4. blow   (brow)

5. spit   (slit, snit)

6. stay   (slay, spay)

7. black

8. spend

9. trip

10. snack   (stack, slack)

Exercise 2

1. This <u>bread</u> is hard.   ✓ bread   ___ bed

2. Did you see my new <u>plants</u>?   ✓ plants   ___ pants

3. That tire looks <u>flat</u>.   ___ flat   ✓ fat

4. He'll <u>break</u> her heart.   ___ break   ✓ bake

5. Let's take the <u>freeway</u>.   ✓ freeway   ___ feeway

6. Can you smell the cookies? ✓ smell ___ sell

7. She has a small plane. ___ plane ✓ pain

8. Can you hear the wind blow? ✓ blow ___ below

9. He plays lots of sports. ___ sports ✓ supports

10. I have a twin sister. ✓ twin ___ to win

Supplement 11. Final Consonant Clusters

Listening Activity 1

wait (waist) (sing) sink (fell) felt

stop (stopped) need (needs) car (card)

(fat) fact (nice) nights mint (minute)

sin (since) (mine) mind (scalp) scallop

Exercise 1

1. ten _t_, ten _s_, ten _d_ 3. wai _s_ t 5. save _d_, save _s_

2. fa _s_ t 4. take _s_ 6. love _d_, love _s_

Exercise 2

1. She got a card on her birthday. ✓ card ___ car

2. They walked every morning. ✓ walked ___ walk

3. They showed me where they work. ___ work ✓ were

4. Did you get new pants? ___ pants ✓ pans

5. I'm calling about the ants in my room. ___ ants ✓ ant

6. That's a fact. ✓ fact ___ fat

7. Are you finished? ___ finished ✓ Finnish

8. Would you make the beds? ___ beds ✓ bed

9. They helped him pay the rent. ✓ helped ___ help

10. He has a beard. ✓ beard ___ beer

Answer Key for Vowel Supplements

Supplement 12. Vowel Phonetic Alphabet

Exercise 1

2	1	13	3
pink	green	white	gray

14	4	5	6
brown	red	black	pu<u>r</u>ple

Supplement 13. Vowel Overview

Exercise 1

1. a. The tongue bunches up in the (front of the mouth, back of the mouth).

b. The tongue bunches up in the (front of the mouth, back of the mouth).

2. a. The lips are (spread, rounded).

b. The lips are (spread, rounded).

3. a. The jaw and the tongue are (high, low).

b. The jaw and the tongue are (high, low).

Exercise 2

Vowel 1: cheese
Vowel 2: sit
Vowel 3: wait
Vowel 4: men
Vowel 5: hat

Exercise 3

Vowel 9: moon
Vowel 10: could
Vowel 11: close
Vowel 12: boss

Exercise 4

Vowel 6: hurt
Vowel 7: /ʌ/bug
        /ə/ <u>A</u>meric<u>a</u>
Vowel 8: socks

Exercise 5

Vowel 13: drive
Vowel 14: loud
Vowel 15: boil

Exercise 6

9
1. conFUSE
5
2. JaPAN
6
3. DIRty
4
4. NoVEMber
1
5. fourTEEN

Exercise 7

ə
1. oc CUR
ə
2. a LONE
ə ə
3. POS si ble
ə
4. com PARE
ə ə
5. tra DI tion

Exercise 8

A: What's the **MAT**ter? [5]

B: I don't know what to wear to **SCHOOL**. [9]

A: Just throw on jeans and a **SHIRT**. [6]

B: But **WHICH** shirt? [2]

A: Your **TEE** shirt. [1]

B: My **BLUE** tee shirt, my **BLACK** tee shirt, my [9] [5]

TIE dye tee shirt, **CON**cert tee shirt, **BASE**ball tee shirt . . .? [13] [8] [3]

A: Just get **DRESSED**! We're going to be **LATE**! [4] [3]

Exercise 11

A or /eʸ/	E or /iʸ/	I or /aɪ/	O or /oʷ/	/uʷ/
late date	clean jeans	arrive alive	slow boat	true blue
same page	sea breeze	bike ride		
gray day	green tea	nice smile		
	cream cheese			

Supplement 15. /iʸ/ heat - /ɪ/ hit

Listening Activity 2

1. eat–it (D)

2. seen–seen (S)

3. heat–hit (D)

4. leap–lip (D)

5. still–still (S)

6. feet–feet (S)

7. heater–heater (S)

8. leave–live (D)

9. feel–fill (D)

Listening Activity 3

1. a. It's cold.

2. b. He likes it.

3. b. They're losing the game.

4. a. In the meadow.

Listening Activity 4

> Counting Sheep
>
> /iʸ/   /iʸ/   /iʸ/
> 1   Many **peo**ple have trouble falling a**slee**p. Some try counting **shee**p.
>   /ɪ/   /iʸ/
> 2   They try to imagine the same **thing** happening over and over, like sheep **lea**ping
>   /ɪ/   /ɪ/
> 3   one after the other. By **thinking** of one thing, they forget other **things**. They
>   /iʸ/
> 4   may actually go to **sleep** because they are bored!

Supplement 16. /eʸ/ late - /ɛ/ let

Listening Activity 2

1. wait–wait (S)

2. test–test (S)

3. main–men (D)

4. pain–pen (D)

5. late–let (D)

6. paper–pepper (D)

7. date–debt (D)

8. whale–whale (S)

9. edge–edge (S)

Listening Activity 3

1. b. No, I paid it off.

2. a. Maybe you should call your doctor.

3. b. Yes. It was easy.

4. a. Aisle 2. With office supplies.

Listening Activity 4

Amazing Trivia

/eʸ/   /ɛ/
1   No piece of <u>paper</u> can be folded more than <u>seven</u> times.
                     /eʸ/
2   The heart of a blue <u>whale</u> is as big as a car.
                              /eʸ/   /eʸ/
3   Women say an average of 7000 words a <u>day</u>; men <u>say</u> just over 2000.
                     /eʸ/
4   The life of a major league <u>baseball</u> is only seven pitches.
         /eʸ/   /eʸ/
5   The <u>main</u> library at Indiana University sinks one inch every year. Engineers <u>failed</u>
                    /eʸ/
    to account for the <u>weight</u> of the books.

Supplement 17. /uʷ/ too - /ʊ/ took

Listening Activity 2

1. fool–full (D)

2. pool–pull (D)

3. Luke–Luke (S)

4. suit–soot (D)

5. who'd–hood (D)

6. stood–stood (S)

Listening Activity 3

Transcript: shoe, put, student, suit, cool, book, should, look, moon, room, would, cook

/uʷ/ – too	/ʊ/ – took
shoe	put
student	book
suit	should
cool	look
moon	would
room	cook

Listening Activity 4

A Cool Hotel

/uʷ/   /ʊ/
1   Do you want to take a <u>cool</u> vacation? How <u>would</u> you like to stay at a hotel
2   where everything is made of ice? At the beautiful Ice Hotel near Quebec
3   City in Canada, the floors, walls, and furniture are made entirely of ice. The
                /uʷ/   /uʷ/
4   hotel has 32 <u>rooms</u>, a wedding chapel, a <u>movie</u> theater, and an ice bar—but
                          /ʊ/
5   no heat. Many people come just to <u>look</u>. If you want to spend the night, you
         /ʊ/   /uʷ/   /uʷ/
6   had better <u>put</u> on your <u>boots</u> and wear a <u>snowsuit</u>!

Supplement 18. /æ/ cap - /ʌ/ cup - /ɑ/ cop

Listening Activity 2

1. cap–cup (D)   **5.** cap–cop (D)   **9.** cup–cop (D)

2. hat–hat (S)   **6.** hat–hot (D)   **10.** hut–hut (S)

3. bag–bug (D)   **7.** odd–odd (S)   **11.** nut–not (D)

4. mad–mud (D)   **8.** Ann–Ann (S)   **12.** lock–lock (S)

Listening Activity 3

Transcript: fact, apple, bun, stuck, hot, dog, not, mad, glad, sad, fun, nuts, love, job, socks

/æ/ cap	/ʌ/ cup	/ɑ/ cop
fact	bun	hot
apple	stuck	dog
mad	fun	not
glad	nuts	job
sad	love	socks

Listening Activity 4

> ### Hot Dogs
>
> /ɑ/ /ɑ/
> 1   Where did we get the name <u>hot dog</u>? The hot part is obvious. Sausages are
>   /ɑ/   /æ/
> 2 <u>hot</u>. In <u>fact</u>, sausages are too hot to hold in your <u>hand</u>, so a baker invented
>   /ʌ/   /ɑ/
> 3 the <u>bun</u>. The dog part is <u>not</u> as obvious. It seems that, in the 1800s, people
>   /ɑ/   /ʌ/
> 4 accused sausage makers of using <u>dog</u> meat. And the name <u>stuck</u>. The first use
>
> 5 of the name *hot dog* was probably in the campus newspaper at Yale University
>   /æ/
> 6 in 1895. Since then, hot dogs have become as American as <u>apple</u> pie.

Index

a, 92
/ɑ/, 19, 187, 188
  central vowel, 189
  simple vowel, 192
  where sound is made, 208
/ɑ/ versus /æ/ versus /ʌ/, 207–210
/æ/, 19, 187
  in *can't*, 96
  front vowel, 188
  simple vowel, 192
  where sound is made, 208
/æ/ versus /ʌ/ versus /ɑ/, 207–210
/aɪ/, 19, 187, 190, 193
and, 92–94
are, 92
Arranging a room, 121–122
as, 92
Aspiration, 157–159
/aʊ/, 19, 187, 190

/b/, 18, 147
  stop, 151, 157–159
  voiced consonant, 25–26, 150
  where sound is made, 153
/b/ versus /p/, 156, 163–165
Branching dialogue, 54
Business card, 32, 42
Business slang and idioms, 94

Campus
  classroom expressions, 83
  radio announcements, 87
  slang and idioms, 51, 63
can, 92
can versus *can't*, 96–97
/tʃ/, 18
  -es after, 37
  making sound, 175
  voiceless consonant, 26, 150
/tʃ/ versus /dʒ/, 156
/tʃ/ versus /dʒ/ versus /ʃ/, 174–177
/tʃ/ versus /ʃ/, 156
/tʃ/ versus /t/, 174
Choice questions, 119
Class notes, 111
Colleges, comparing, 100–101
Comma, with thought group, 127
Compound nouns, stressed syllables in, 64–66
Connected speech, 133–146. *See also* Linking
Consonants
  continuants, 151
  final, 21–30, 163–166
  final clusters, 184–186
  initial, 157–161
  initial clusters, 181–183
  linking, 134–138
  phonetic alphabet, 147–148
  stops, 151, 157–161
  symbols, 18
  voiced, 25–26, 149–150
  voiceless, 25–26, 149–150
Content words, 82–83
Continuants, 151

/d/, 18, 147
  -ed ending, 46–47
  linking with, 141–143
  stop, 151, 157–159
  voiced consonant, 25–26, 150
  where sound is made, 154

/d/ versus /t/, 156, 163–165
Dates, 173
Dialogue
  branching, 54
  finish the conversation, 98
Dictionary
  pronunciation symbols in, 17–19
  stress syllables in, 15–16
  syllable separation in, 13
  uses for, 11
Diphthongs, 190–191
Dot (•), above focus in thought group, 128
/dʒ/, 18
  /d/ + /y/ as, 143
  -es after, 37
  making sound, 175
  voiced consonant, 26, 150
/dʒ/ versus /tʃ/, 156
/dʒ/ versus /tʃ/ versus /ʃ/, 174–177

/ɛ/, 19, 187
  front vowel, 188
  no movement with, 193
  simple vowel, 192
/ɛ/ versus /eʸ/, 199–202
-ed, 43–52
/eɪ/, 19
English language, most beautiful words in, 14
-er, 70
/ɝ/, 19, 187
  central vowel, 189
  simple vowel, 192
-es, 37
/eʸ/, 19, 187
  front vowel, 188
  glided vowel, 192
  movement with, 193
/eʸ/ versus /ɛ/, 199–202

/f/, 18, 147
  continuant, 151
  voiceless consonant, 25–26, 150
  where sound is made, 153
Fable, "The Old Man and His Sons," 50
Fears, 186
/fɚ/, 92
Flavors, 177
Focus words, 99–112
  changes in focus, 105–110
  to disagree or correct, 112
  movement with, 108
  normal focus, 102–104
  pitch change with, 101
  vowel in, 191
Focus, dot (•) above, in thought group, 128
for, 92
-ful, 70
Full forms, 91
Function words
  full forms, 91
  reduced forms, 91
  reduced words, 89–90
  unstressed, 82, 85

/g/, 18, 147
  stop, 151, 157–159
  voiced consonant, 25–26, 150
  where sound is made, 154

/g/ versus /k/, 163–164
Goal setting, 7–10

/h/, 18, 147
  not paired, 26, 150
  where sound is made, 154
had, 95
has, 95
have, 92, 95
he, 95
her, 92, 95
he's, 95
him, 92, 95
his, 95
Homonyms, 48

/ɪ/, 19, 187
  front vowel, 188
  no movement with, 193
  reduced forms, 91
  simple vowel, 192
  where sound is made, 196
/ɪ/ versus /iʸ/, 195–198
-ian, 70, 72
-ic, 70–71
-ical, 71
/ɪd/, 46–47
Idioms
  business, 94
  campus, 51, 63
/ɪm/, 92
in, 92
/ɪn/, 92
Instructions, giving, 130–132
Interview questions, 4
Intonation, 113–122
  end of statement, 115
  question, 113
  rising, 116
Introduction, making, 5
-ion, 70–71
-ity, 70–71
/iʸ/, 19, 187
  front vowel, 188
  glided vowel, 192
  movement with, 193
  where sound is made, 196
/iʸ/ versus /i/, 195–198
/ɪz/, 36–37

Job interview, 99

/k/, 18, 147
  stop, 151, 157–161
  voiceless consonant, 25–26, 150
  where sound is made, 154
/k/ versus /g/, 163–164
/kn/, 92, 96
/kən/, 92, 96

/l/, 18, 147
  frontal view of, 179
  saggital view of, 179
  where sound is made, 154
/l/ versus /r/, 156, 178–180
Language, rhythm of, 85
Laws, strange, 210
Linking
  consonant to vowel, 134–136, 138
  /d/ to /y/, 143
  -ed sound to next word, 48–49
  final consonant sound, 24–25
  same consonant sounds, 136–138

-s ending to next word, 39–40
  /t/ sounds, 141–142
  vowel-to-vowel, 139
Lip-reading exercise, 28

/m/, 18, 147
  where sound is made, 153
/m/ versus /n/, 156
/m/ versus /n/ versus /ŋ/, 166–169
Meal planning, 198
-ment, 70
Mental practice, 111

/n/, 18, 147
  reduced form, 92
  where sound is made, 154
/n/ versus /m/ 156
/n/ versus /m/ versus /ŋ/, 166–169
/ŋ/, 18
  where sound is made, 154
/ŋ/ versus /n/ versus /m/, 166–169
-ness, 70
New Year's resolutions, 183
Newbury House Dictionary, 16
Nouns
  compound, stressed syllables in, 64–66
  two-syllable, stress in, 58–59
Noun-verb pairs, stressed syllables in, 59–60
Numbers, *-teen*, 57

Odd jobs, 41
of, 92–94
"Old Man and His Sons, The," 50
or, 92
Oral presentation, 76–78
/oʊ/, 19
/oʷ/, 187
  back vowel, 189
  glided vowel, 192
  movement with, 193
/ɔ/, 19, 187
  back vowel, 189
  no movement with, 193
  simple vowel, 192
/ɔɪ/, 19, 187, 189

/p/, 18, 147
  stop, 151, 157–161
  voiceless consonant, 25–26, 150
  where sound is made, 153
/p/ versus /b/, 156, 163–165
Paragraph, reading, 2, 75
Past tense. *See* Present or past
Pausing, thought groups and, 123–132
Period, with thought group, 127
Personal word list, 20, 78
Personality, sleep positions and, 67–68
Phobias, 186
Picture story, 3
Poem, "This Is Just to Say," (Williams), 88
Post-it™ notes, 88
Practice
  mental, 111
  slow-motion, 27
Present or past (tense), 44–45, 144

Presentation
    giving instructions, 130–132
    oral, 76–78
Pronunciation, 1–6
    basics, 8
    checklist, 6
    goals for, 7–10
    practice for, 27
    self-monitoring, 74
Pronunciation key, 18–19
Pronunciation pyramid, 9
Pronunciation scale, 10
Pronunciation symbols, 17–19

Questions
    answering, 4
    asking, 145–146
    choice, 119
    interview, 4
    returned, 117–118
    wh-, 105, 113–117
    yes/no, 113, 117

/r/, 18, 147
    frontal view of, 179
    saggital view of, 179
    where sound is made, 154
/r/ versus /l/, 156, 178–180
Reduced forms, 91
Reduced words, 89–98. *See also*
    Function words
Requests, making, 145
Resolutions, New Year's, 183
Returned questions, 117–118
Rhymes, 84
Rhythm
    defined, 79
    with reduced words, 89–98
    See also Rhythm-stressed
    words
Rhythm-stressed words, 79–88
Room, arranging, 121–122

/s/, 18, 147
    continuant, 151
    ending, 36–37, 40
    voiceless consonant, 25–26,
    150, 171
    where sound is made, 154
/s/ versus /ʃ/, 174
/s/ versus /θ/, 156, 170–172
-s, 31–42
    linking to next word, 39–40
    omitting, 35
    pronouncing, 36–37
Schedule, 202
/ə/ (Schwa), 19
    central vowel, 189
    reduced form, 91–94
    unstressed syllable, 61, 73, 96,
    187, 191
/əm/, 92
/ən/, 92, 94
/ər/, 92
/əv/, 92
/əz/, 36–37, 40, 86, 92
Self-monitoring, 74
Sentences, thought groups in, 126
/ʃ/, 18
    -es after, 37
    voiceless consonant, 26, 150,
    175
    where sound is made, 154
/ʃ/ versus /s/, 174
/ʃ/ versus /tʃ/, 156
/ʃ/ versus /tʃ/ versus /dʒ/,
    174–177

Slang
    business, 94
    campus, 51, 63
Slash (/), at end of thought group,
    123–128
Sleep positions, 67–68
Slow-motion practice, 27
Song lyrics
    hidden words in, 136
    website, 98
Spring break vacation, 169
Stops, 151, 157–161
Stress
    primary, 15–17
    rhythm and, 79–88
    secondary, 16
Stressed syllables, 53–66
    compound nouns, 64–66
    noun-phrasal verb pairs, 62
    stressing wrong syllable, 55
    strong syllable, 56, 69
    suffixes, 67–78
    -teen numbers, 57
    two-syllable nouns, 58–59
    two-syllable verbs, 58–59
    vowels and, 61
Suffixes, 67–78
Syllables, 11–17
    defined, 11
    and *-ed* endings, 43–52
    number of, in word, 11–12
    omitting, 13
    and *-s* endings, 31–42
    stressed, 15. *See also* Stressed
    syllables
Symbol
    pronunciation, 17–19. *See also*
    Pronunciation symbols *and*
    entries for specific symbols
    slash (/), 123–128
    stress, 15–17
    voiced consonants, 149–150

/t/, 18, 147
    -ed ending, 46–47
    linking with, 141–142
    stop, 151, 157–161
    voiceless consonant, 25–26,
    150, 171
    where sound is made, 154
/t/ versus /d/, 156, 163–165
/t/ versus /tʃ/, 174
/t/ versus /θ/, 170–172
/tə/, 92, 94
-teen numbers, 57
Telephone message, 21–22, 30
/θ/, 18
    voiceless consonant, 26, 150,
    171
    where sound is made, 153
/θ/ versus /s/, 156, 170–172
/θ/ versus /t/, 170–172
/ð/, 18
    voiced consonant, 26, 150
    where sound is made, 153
"This Is Just to Say," (Williams),
    88
Thought groups
    comma with, 127
    defined, 125
    dot (•) above focus in, 128
    giving instructions and, 130–
    132
    pausing and, 123–132
    period with, 127
    slash (/) at end of, 123–128
Time, 173

Timelines, 52
to, 92, 94
TOEFL® iBT Practices, 51, 120
Travel game, 65

/u/, 19
/ʊ/, 19, 187
    back vowel, 189
    no movement with, 193
    simple vowel, 192
    where sound is made, 204
/ʊ/ versus /uʷ/, 203–206
/uʷ/, 19, 187, 188
    back vowel, 189
    glided vowel, 192
    movement with, 193
    stressed syllable, 61
    where sound is made, 204
/uʷ/ versus /ʊ/, 203–206
/ʌ/, 19, 187
    central vowel, 189
    simple vowel, 192
    where sound is made, 208
/ʌ/ versus /æ/ versus /ɑ/,
    207–210

/v/, 18, 147
    reduced form, 92
    voiced consonant, 25–26, 150
    where sound is made, 153
Verbs, two-syllable, stress in,
    58–59
Vowel chart, 190
Vowels
    back, 189, 204–205
    central, 189, 208–209
    diphthongs, 190–191
    in focus word, 191
    front, 188, 196, 200, 208–209
    glided, 192–193
    linking, 139. *See also* Linking
    making vowel sounds, 188–
    191
    phonetic alphabet, 187
    simple, 192–193
    in stressed syllables, 61
    in unstressed syllables, 61, 191
Vowel sound
    in syllable, 11
    before voiced consonants, 25
Vowel symbols, 19

/w/, 18, 147
    not paired, 26, 150
    vowel sounds linked by,
    139–140
    where sound is made, 153
Wh-questions, 105, 113–117
Williams, William Carlos, 88
Words
    content, 82–83
    focus, 99–112
    function, 82, 85, 89–92
    reduced, 89–98
    rhythm-stressed, 79–88
would/wouldn't do, 206

/y/, 18, 147
    linking /d/ to, 143
    not paired, 26, 150
    vowel sounds linked by,
    139–140
    where sound is made, 154
Yes/no questions, 113, 117
/yuʷ/, 193

/z/, 18, 147
    ending, 36–37, 40

    as voiced consonant, 25–26,
    150
    where sound is made, 154
/ʒ/, 18
    -es after, 37
    voiced consonant, 26, 150
    where sound is made, 154